TRANSF
LEADERSHIP:
AN ETHNOGRAPHIC STUDY OF PRINCIPALS' INFLUENCE ON INSTRUCTIONAL EFFECTIVENESS OF TEACHING ENGLISH LANGUAGE LEARNERS IN SELECT ELEMENTARY SCHOOLS

Christie M. Petersen, Ed.D.

TRANSFORMATIONAL LEADERSHIP:
AN ETHNOGRAPHIC STUDY OF PRINCIPALS'
INFLUENCE ON INSTRUCTIONAL EFFECTIVENESS
OF TEACHING ENGLISH LANGUAGE LEARNERS
IN SELECT ELEMENTARY SCHOOLS

You can write to the author at cpetersen@corban.edu.

Presented to Educational Foundations and Leadership Department
George Fox University, Newberg, Oregon
In Partial Fulfillment of the Requirements
For the Degree of Doctor of Educational Leadership

Additional copies of this volume are available for sale online at
www.BooksaMillion.com
www.BarnesandNoble.com
www.Amazon.com

ABSTRACT

This qualitative study was designed to gain an in-depth understanding of the role of the principal in successfully improving English Language Learner (ELL) educational outcomes in high poverty schools based on interviews with five elementary principals who were employed by Hillsboro School District during the SET-R grant from school years 2007-2010.

Three questions guided this study. First, how do the principals promote or implement school culture expectations and best instructional practices in elementary schools with high ELL populations? Second, what level of general knowledge about leadership characteristics do the principals possess whose students performed well academically as measured by OAKS in elementary schools with high ELL populations? Third, what do the principals regard as an effective approaches to comprehensively serve ELL populations?

The interviews were in a semi-structured format and were designed to allow the participant opportunities to discuss professional experiences.

This topic continues to be a concern for administrators given the persistent achievement gap between ELLs and their peers at the secondary level despite some gains in the primary grade levels.

In analyzing the themes it became evident that leadership characteristics are perceived as specific skills that principals acquire through experiences only which are necessary to move schools through the change process.

Some of the challenges faced were the lack of knowledge about the principal's impact on second language acquisition, lack of leadership coaching, and lack of common agreements about which best practices to use.

Moreover, there appeared to be lack of agreement between the participants and other administrators about what important actions a principal takes to ensure full implementation of ELL initiatives such as English Language Development (ELD).

ACKNOWLEDGMENTS

I would like to dedicate this research project to my husband, Paul, and to my children, Andrew, Rachael and Aaron, who have been my constant support throughout this journey as I sought to do God's will in my life as an educator and administrator.

They encouraged me to become the best principal, district level administrator, teacher, and researcher possible. They all sacrificed and spent many hours without wife and mom present while I was doing research or writing.

My children were patient with mom having to do homework in the evening and on weekends. They were helpful in bringing me tea, flowers, and a kind word about how exciting graduation would be for us all.

My husband helped me with technology needs, read my manuscript, offered many helpful suggestions, and made sure that I kept a promise I had made twenty years ago. He modeled God's faithfulness and unconditional love.

I would also like to dedicate my work to my mom, Margie, who, from a very early age, reminded me that with Jesus Christ I can do all things and has been the wind beneath my wings since before the time I could read or write. Her constant love and support has helped to keep all of the home fires burning no matter what deadline I was facing.

I want to thank my mentors, Tony Cox and Brenda Kephart. You taught me how to "keep on keeping on" no matter what came my way. You both were amazing models for a new administrator.

I was inspired to begin and finish this project to improve the work with ELL students by Evelyn Nash Hall. Ev, I miss you terribly and can still hear your voice saying, "We are smart enough to figure it out for our students. We will do whatever it takes." I watched your determination to make a difference.

Lastly, a huge thank you goes to Dr. Marc Shelton, who was always positive, patient, and supportive. He constantly supported my work and made the learning process enjoyable.

Also, thanks to Dr. Scot Headley and Dr. Steve Song for their exceptional words of advice, insight, and professional suggestions.

TABLE OF CONTENTS

LIST OF FIGURES

CHAPTER 1

INTRODUCTION

Public schools in America continue to undertake the momentous task of educating all students who arrive at the door of each classroom to become college and career ready irrespective of their ethnicity, religious background, and/ or financial standing.

Administrators and teachers are presented with the task of creating healthy and competent school systems in a culture that ensures the success of students as a result of instruction built upon the strengths of each child.

The teacher is part of the team responsible for setting up these systems, while it is the principal who is held most accountable for student outcomes in a school (Reeves, 2004).

There continues to be an appropriate and intense focus on student performance indicators including Special Education and ethnic subgroups as required by the No Child Left Behind (NCLB) Act of 2001.

The current administration's College and Career Ready emphasis is forthcoming with the recent ESEA Flexibility Waiver applications to be completed by each state early in 2012 holding states accountable for student outcomes according to United States Department of Education.

It is imperative that America's schools operate in such a manner that keeping a close eye on subgroup data for Special

Education, English Language Learners (ELLs), and high poverty students is part of their daily work. Gathering such data, noting which students are not at grade level, and using immediate assessment tools to gather data for placement into specific interventions, is imperative for principals to effectively lead and support teachers who are empowered to design rigorous, high yield instructional interventions in order to assist in closing the achievement gap and to avoid missing opportunities for student catch-up growth as a result of "organizational clutter" (Elmore, 2000).

Several studies have been conducted concerning the comparison between English Language Learners' poor performance and the performance of their peers (Baca, Fletcher, and Hoover, 2008; Betts, Reuben, and Danenberg, 2000; Gersten and Baker, 2000). As a result, the emphasis on necessary changes in teaching and leadership practices for both elementary and secondary schools in the past six to eight years has shifted drastically to a focus specifically on English Language Learners.

Researchers at the Center for Advancement of Racial and Ethnic Equity (2010) recently completed a study that provided a necessary structure to ensure positive educational outcomes for all students as educators strive to make significant systemic changes. Recommendations indicated a need for teachers and administrators to use a process for data-driven decision making, to develop a strong sense of collective responsibility for ensuring an equitable education for all students, and to increase awareness of inequalities in schools.

It is the principal leadership that truly matters in providing this structure for student success (Marzano, Waters, and McNulty, 2005). In *School Leadership That Works,* researchers Robert Marzano, Timothy Waters, and Brian McNulty propose a plan for strong and thoughtful leadership to allow for second-order change or deep change that will make a "profound difference" in student achievement results. "The need for truly effective educational leadership is great. The time for improving our schools is short. The opportunity to lead is ours…the only thing left is to act" (2005).

It is in this changing landscape of accountability that district and building level administrators and teachers in Hillsboro School District found themselves five years ago. School personnel were struggling to establish viable solutions for closing the persistent achievement gap for their English Language Learner students from grades K-12.

Closing the achievement gap for ELLs is still an intense focus in 2011 in Hillsboro as the main District initiatives and resources are being allocated towards that end because the gap beyond grade three for ELLs has shown few gains towards closing and the Special Education students for Hillsboro were still outperforming the ELLs on state assessments.

However, some strides were made to increase the performance of ELLs at grade three to nearly 70% of the students through the work of an early literacy initiative call Reading First. Hillsboro did see significant changes in closing the achievement gap in reading from Kindergarten to third grade for all students including Hispanic students.

Many of the schools' passing rates at grade three were near 32% in 2003 for the highest poverty schools in Hillsboro, which lead to being invited by the Oregon Department of Education to participate in the first round of Reading First grants. Unfortunately, the gains have not been sustained from grade four to graduation at 12th grade where a 23-point gap exists between White and Hispanic students and a 60-point gap exists between White students and students receiving ELL services (see Figure 1).

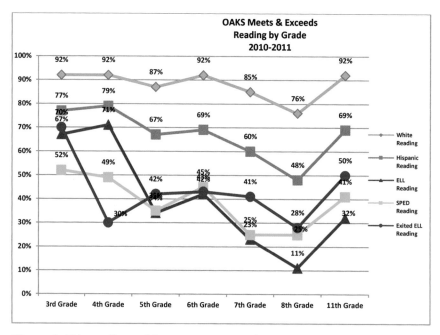

Figure 1: ELL reading achievement gap in the Hillsboro School District.

The current trends in Hillsboro's graduation rates show that fewer than 40% of English Language Learner students make it to graduation.

Using these current figures, approximately 1800 of the estimated 2803 students who currently qualify for ELL services in Hillsboro would not graduate from high school if the District did not aggressively pursue other instructional programs such as native language instruction, dual language instruction, or SET-R research grant strategies known as Systematic Explicit Teaching Routines to change graduation outcomes.

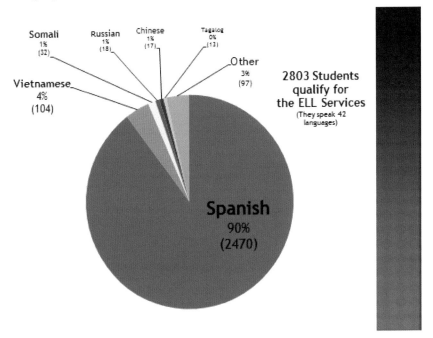

Figure 2: Number of students in Hillsboro School District that qualify as ELL.

Through the pursuit of additional instructional programs, in less than four years' time, Hillsboro reports a graduation rate of 91.5% which surpasses the state average of 76.5% as tracked by Oregon Department of Education in 2011. This data is easily accessed from the District's website along with specific information for all stakeholders about how the District is going to continue to focus intensely on meeting the needs of all students, especially for ELLs where a persistent achievement gap remains and many of these Hispanic students are dropping out of high school prior to graduation. This focus will be done in a dedicated pursuit of the District's mission to "[e]ngage and challenge all learners to ensure academic success" (2011).

Understanding the demographics of the Hillsboro School District is important because it has changed drastically in the past fifteen years. Along with population changes has come the need for changing instructional practices by educators in the school district.

According to the Hillsboro Chamber of Commerce, Hillsboro can be described as big town of over 200 square miles that has a little town feel or small-town charm. While it is mostly known for its high tech industry with Intel fabrication facilities throughout the city, farming and timber businesses remain as well.

As one of the oldest communities in Washington County in the state of Oregon, Hillsboro has seen a huge growth in population in the past decade with many of those families being Hispanic (2011).

Hillsboro School District currently serves close to 21,000 students in programs offered in 35 elementary and secondary schools.

Of those students, 53% are White, 33% are Hispanic, 7% are Asian/Pacific Islander, 3.3 % are Multi-Ethnic, and 2.1 % are Black according to the District's website (2012).

There are 42 languages that are spoken in Hillsboro School District. English is spoken by 68% of the students, while 26% of the students speak Spanish (see Figure 3).

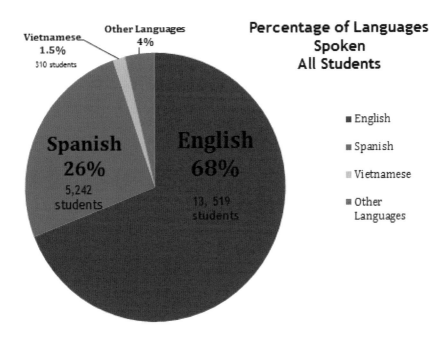

Figure 3: Percentage of spoken languages in Hillsboro School District in 2011.

One of the promising instructional strategies that the District initially used in an attempt to close the achievement gap for ELL students was done through a partnership with Drs. Scott and Doris Baker from the University of Oregon and the Pacific Institutes for Research that began in the fall of 2007.

Hillsboro School District (HSD) became a participating district with five elementary schools being studied for Oregon, and 25 schools from Texas in the Bakers' federally funded research project entitled *Reading Intervention with Spanish-Speaking Students: Maximizing Instructional Effectiveness in English and Spanish (SET-R)*.

The purpose of the research was to "test the efficacy of an instructional approach designed to increase the early literacy achievement of Spanish-speaking English language learners in transitional bilingual education programs" (Baker and Baker, 2007).

Dr. Doris Baker selected Hillsboro to participate in this grant opportunity as a result of the careful implementation of the Reading First Grants by the teachers, principals, and district level administrators and the University of Oregon during the previous four years, which yielded significant achievement results for ELL students in grades K-3 (see Figure 1).

I was personally involved as part of the District Title I administrative team who wrote the Reading First grants and supervised the implementation of the training and work. We were thrilled with an opportunity to take what we had learned about early literacy for monolingual English speakers to see if we could build upon the explicit teaching routines in English by transferring the same strategies to native language instruction in Spanish to improve outcomes for our emerging bilingual students.

Immediately upon invitation, Hillsboro accepted the opportunity to partner and begin the work of the SET-R grant. The SET-R grant research was conducted for three years. Five of the highest poverty, Title I elementary schools in HSD with approximately 2500 students total, over 30% of whom were ELLs, were selected for the study that occurred from the beginning of the 2007 school year and to the end of the school year in June of 2010.

The SET-R grant provided training, strategies, and programs that helped our ELL students make significant learning gains. The principals in each of these schools played a critical role in the success of these students. During this time, three of these five schools were able to remain out of NCLB Sanctions altogether and two of the five schools that went into sanctions were able to transform rapidly and successfully enough to be removed from the list of schools in sanctions as tracked by Oregon Department of Education (2011).

The work that Hillsboro did with the SET-R grant was timely and helpful for the students in those schools. Principal leadership was an important component to the overall success of the implementation of the instructional strategies being studied by the SET-R researchers.

In 2012, Hillsboro is in a different place politically and philosophically because eleven years have passed since the Bush administration worked with Congress to pass the NCLB Act. Re-authorization of this law is now overdue and waivers from federal regulations were being considered at the state level early in the fall of 2011 with submission of the waivers to the federal level during the early winter of 2012 (Brownstein, 2011).

Recent research about school transformation has emphasized the impact of teacher quality as a primary factor in determining levels of specific student achievement (Marzano, 2003).

Additionally, the research on principal leadership indicates the school principal may have more of a direct influence on the academic achievement of students within a school than was previously supposed, specifically with regard to ELL students (Aleman, Johnson and Perez, 2009; Goldenberg, 2004; Heck and Hallinger, 2005; and Marzano, Waters, and McNulty, 2005).

A meta-analysis completed by Robert Marzano and colleagues from Mid-continent Research for Education and Learning (McREL) in 2004 claims that 35 years of research offers clear guidance on "specific leadership behaviors" and provides plenty of documentation that those characteristics have an "effect on student achievement." (Marzano, Waters, and McNulty, 2005).

District leadership for Hillsboro knew from the outcome of student performance data from the SET-R schools that something positive was occurring as a result of effective principal leadership on student achievement. Marzano, Waters, and McNulty were able to show a statistically significant correlation between their list of The 21 Leadership Responsibilities of a School Leader and student academic achievement outcomes.

Two questions need to be explored through further study. First, are all of the 21 responsibilities or characteristics identified by Marzano necessary in order for a leader to impact student achievement for ELLs? Second, are there are certain principal characteristics from the list of 21 or from personal experience that are more important than others related to having an overall positive impact on ELL student achievement?

Although the numbers of ELL students continue to grow rapidly in Hillsboro and the United States, studies such as Marzano's work with McREL, Cotton's work, and a final synthesis study by Leithwood and colleagues suggest there is a correlation between leadership abilities and student achievement. Marzano's study yielded the list of The 21 Leadership Responsibilities and suggests a plan for team leadership to ensure that all areas are employed in a school to ensure positive student outcomes (Marzano et al., 2005).

Kathy Cotton conducted a narrative review called *Principals and Student Achievement: What the Research Says* in 2003. After reviewing over 85 reports, she indicated there were 25 categories of "principal behavior that positively affect the dependent variables of student achievement" (Cotton, 2003).

Cotton's list of 25 categories is similar to Marzano's list of The 21 Leadership Responsibilities.

While the research does show that the principal has an indirect influence on student achievement, it is considered "second only to classroom instruction among all school-related factors that contribute to what students learn at school" according to *Investigating the Links to Improved Student Learning* (Wahlstrom, Louis, Leithwood, and Anderson, 2010).

What perceived influence the principal has on student achievement for ELLs specifically is still undetermined at this time due to the finding from the previous research that "both principal and teacher leadership that is focused on improving student learning decreases as poverty and diversity increase" (Wahlstrom et al., 2010). What is disturbing about this finding is that many ELL students consistently attend the highest poverty schools.

Determining what specific successful school leadership characteristics from the list of The 21 Leadership Responsibilities is important because according to the Wallace Foundation's recent study *The School Principal as Leader*, the principal does the work of creating conditions under which important school variables get combined to reach a "critical mass" in order for school improvement to occur for students.

The perceptions of principals who were successful with ELLs in their school and which leadership traits were important to their school improvement efforts through the SET-R grant merits further study.

Statement of the Problem

The purpose of this research endeavor was to investigate the role of the principal in improving English Language Learners (ELL) academic outcomes and to examine more closely successful school leadership traits of principals in schools with high ELL populations to identify what the specific traits or characteristics look like.

The framework guide for this research was Marzano, Waters, and McNulty's *The 21 Leadership Responsibilities List.* The researcher used the list as a starting place in identifying possible leadership characteristics among a purposive sample of principals who worked for the Hillsboro School District during the SET-R grant.

Specifically, the researcher used personal interviews as a means to investigate the principal leadership characteristics associated with leading a school where ELL students had high achievement scores.

An objective of this study was to gain greater understanding about which characteristics already listed in previous research—or not listed but a part of personal experience mentioned by the principals interviewed—were related to change that made them successful at their respective school with a high percentage of ELL students.

Research Questions

Because the intent of this study is exploratory, the following research questions were created to encourage dialogue between the interviewer and the participant.

However, the questions were designed with a theme towards investigating the knowledge base of effective principal leadership characteristics and how those characteristics made the principal successful leading improved performance within the ELL population of a school.

The following three research questions were selected to guide this specific research.

Research Question #1:

How do the principals promote or implement school culture expectations and best instructional practices in elementary schools with high populations of ELL students?

Research Question #2:

What level of general knowledge about leadership elements and characteristics do the principals possess whose students performed well academically as measured by OAKS (Oregon Assessment of Knowledge and Skills test) in elementary schools with high populations of ELL students?

Research Question #3:

What do the principals perceive as an effective approach or approaches to comprehensively serve ELL students in grades K-6?

Definition of Terms

- *Effective Behavioral and Instructional Support Systems (EBISS):* Through the application of a blended model of response to intervention (RTI) and positive behavioral interventions and supports, districts and programs will be able to meet the academic and behavioral needs of every student in their schools or programs (Oregon Department of Education, 2010).

- *English Language Development (ELD):* Instruction in English language as its own course of study for students (Dutro, 2005).

- *English Language Learners:* Students who speak English either not at all or with several limitations that they cannot fully participate in mainstream English instruction (Aleman, Johnson Jr. and Perez, 2009).

- *Elementary Secondary Education Act (ESEA) Act:* Legislation that was passed in 1965 as an effort to fight the war on poverty in America's schools. It establishes high accountability and emphasizes equal access to rigorous instruction for all students. Includes Title IA (Improving Basic Education for At-risk Students, Title ID (Neglected and Delinquent), and Title X (McKinney-Vento Act for students living in homeless situations). The Bush Administration reauthorized it in 2001 as the No Child Left Behind (NCLB) Act. (ED.gov, 2011).

- *Response to Intervention:* Schools identify students at risk for poor learning outcomes, monitor student progress, provide evidence-base interventions and adjust the intensity and nature of those interventions depending on a student's responsiveness, and identify students with learning disabilities or other disabilities (NCRTI, 2010).

- *SET-R Program: Systematic, Explicit Teaching Routines:* A set of field-tested teaching templates developed by researchers at the Center for Teaching and Learning to aid in the investigation of whether enhancing core reading instruction improves the immediate and long term Spanish and English literacy achievement of English-language learners in first and second grade in 48 schools in Texas and Oregon (CTL, 2011).

- *Transformational Leadership Skills:* A style of leadership focused on producing unexpected but necessary results. Leaders possess the Four I's of leadership: individual consideration, intellectual stimulation, inspirational motivation, and idealized influence (Waters, 2005).

Limitations and Delimitations

The researcher in this study focused specifically on enhancing the understanding of the principal behavior and characteristics as defined by the five building level administrators in each of the five Hillsboro School District schools that were included in the SET-R grant.

The use of existing theory from Marzano, Waters, and McNulty's meta-analysis published as *School Leadership that Works: From Research to Results* (2004) was the framework guide for this project. The List of 21 Leadership Responsibilities or Characteristics (see Appendix C) was used in refining the interview schedule into a smaller set of focused questions.

The conceptualization of the key concepts or variables for this research began with the framework as a guide, but allowed for discovery of other potential major variables.

The interview schedule, the researcher's questioning techniques and the way that the questions were written intentionally allowed for the discovery of additional principal characteristics that may relate to student successes that may not have been identified or included from previous research.

It was the goal of the researcher to use the existing theory as a "spotlight" that could help to illuminate this particular area of principal leadership, knowing that the risk might be to overlook another area unintentionally if the survey instrument did not allow for discovery from the responses provided by participants (Maxwell, 2005).

Due to the small research sample size of this exploratory, qualitative study, the ability to generalize the findings is limited. It is not the goal of the researcher to try to understand all the facets of the highly complex nature of the role of the principals and student outcomes in their schools, but it is hoped that this research will illuminate some of the successful leadership characteristics of principals who are most effective with ELLs based on the principals' personal perspectives and reflections on the meaning of their lives and experiences as principals.

This research will be difficult to replicate because the principals have retired and new leadership in their schools appears to have already had an impact by shifting focus away from explicit instruction and toward dual language instruction.

The interviews were conducted in late December 2011 and in January 2012 to accommodate the work schedules of both the candidates and the researcher.

All participants were involved in post-retirement work, either coaching as an employee of Oregon Department of Education or offering consulting services to other school districts.

Interview characteristics of the five interviewees such as age, sex, and race were limited in this study and could lead to a result of biased responses.

The other twenty-one elementary schools in Hillsboro School District were not included in this study because they did not participate in the SET-R grant.

Targeting the Systematic, Explicit Teaching Routines (SET-R) schools in this study and using a purposive sampling technique is an important parameter because the types of school improvement plans that were in place at the SET-R schools were similar. These plans were approved by the Oregon Department of Education and aligned with Hillsboro School District's Consolidated Improvement Plan required by Title IA for school-wide supplemental programs and federal funding. Schools that were included in the SET-R study in the Hillsboro School District, whose principals have not retired, were not included in this study, which may directly or indirectly affect this study due to the fact that new administration at the district level has discontinued Hillsboro's research with the University of Oregon and Pacific Institutes for Research.

The discontinuation of the District's partnership with the SET-R researchers was due to a philosophical shift in the District's approach to closing the achievement gap for ELLs to a more intense focus on dual language programs as the viable solution.

The remaining two principals who participated in SET-R are currently employed with the District and are heavily involved in the new initiatives.

All five retired principals whose schools participated in the SET-R grant consented to interviews for the purposes of this research project.

CHAPTER 2

REVIEW OF THE LITERATURE

This chapter presents a very brief history of the population growth of English Language Learners (ELLs) in the United States as a way to establish the context for a discussion on the prevailing ELL achievement gap dilemma.

Subsequent to this discussion, the researcher describes the literature on why principal leadership matters in closing achievement gap for ELLs.

Included in this examination is a consideration of which of The 21 Leadership Responsibilities or Characteristics may considered as high leverage skills for all principals to master in order to win their schools for ELLs in addition to sharing other promising leadership characteristics.

Brief History of the Population Growth of ELL

Multiple sets of data from the U.S. Department of Education shows increased emphasis on English Language Learners in school improvement efforts (2011). This focus is a result of the pressure for accountability that was created by NCLB mandates and state policies designed to address the dramatic population increase of immigrants to the United States.

In 1993-1994, there were two million ELL students receiving services in public schools in the United States (11% of all students) and five million students in the 2004-2005 school year. It was estimated that the number of students classified as ELL would shift from one in nine students (11%) to one in four (25%) in the "near future" according to Goldenberg in 2004.

Recently, according to the USDOE Institute for Educational Sciences National Center for Educational Statistics, Goldenberg's prediction from 2004-2005 school year was correct. In the 2010-2011 school year, 21% of the students (11.2 million) were classified as ELL (2011).

This explosive growth of ELLs is in stark contrast to the fact that the overall school population has grown less than 3% from 1998-2008 while the ELL student population has increased by more than 60% in that same frame according to the United States Department of Education's (USDoE) report in 2008.

The number of students needing support in ELL programs during those 10 years increased by 25% from 3,643,219 students to 4,492,068 students (Linquanti, 2011). In 2000, California State Department of Education reported having over 1.4 million Limited English Proficiency (LEP) students, which was the highest in the nation. This is over 41% of the total number of ELL students in the United States. Other states, like Nevada and North Carolina, estimate their ELL populations have grown over 200% to 500% (U.S. Department of Education, 2008). In addition, USDOE reports that 80% of these ELL students speak Spanish although there are over 400 different languages spoken (2008).

Not only is the large size of this growing population a challenge, but the differing levels of language proficiencies has had a huge impact on programs and resources. These students need to learn a new language in conjunction with learning basic content standards all in the course of the school day over their school career (Linquanti, 2011).

Today's principals, teachers, and aspiring administrators will need to have refined leadership characteristics and abilities to impact this changing student population more effectively than their predecessors were able to do or were required to do (Wong, 2000), thus changing the role of the principal even more drastically in their efforts to support teaching and learning.

ELL Populations and the Achievement Gap Issue

Researchers, educators, administrators, and politicians agree that the persistent academic achievement gap, especially at the secondary level (see Figure 1), between the English learners and the native English speakers can be a huge challenge to overcome (Witziers, 2003).

It is important to note that on the 2007 National Assessment of Education Progress (NAEP), students who were not native speakers of English scored 36 points below their native English speaking peers in fourth and eighth grade, and that nonnative speakers of English scored even further behind with a 42-point gap in twelfth grade. This achievement gap is significant.

Students who are successful academically can and do earn

a high school diploma and that graduation rates can be predicted by fourth grade reading assessments while success at this grade level is dependent on skills students learned in Kindergarten and first grade (Powell-Smith, Good, and Atkins, 2010). In addition, first grade vocabulary can predict fourth grade reading outcomes (Juel, 1988, see Figure 4).

Both principals and teachers at the elementary level have the responsibility and a moral imperative to ensure that the American dream of being a self-reliant individual and productive member of society becomes a reality for all students by providing access to well-trained teachers, rigorous curriculum, accelerated intervention programs, and comprehensive English Language Development (ELD) instruction (Riveria, 2009; Carr, 2006; Snow, 1998; Coulter, 2009).

The repercussions for ELLs with the persistent elementary achievement gap and the ever widening secondary achievement gap are that these students are on a trajectory for dropping out of school before they reach grade nine.

One study, conducted by the National Center for Education Statistics (NCES) in 2003, found that the dropout rate for Latino students ages 16-19 was 25% compared to 6% for Caucasian students and 10% for African American students. Students' limited English proficiency could be a contributing factor to the higher percentage of dropouts among Latino students.

Nearly 80% of the ELLs speak Spanish as their native language, however achievement tests and classroom instruction are given in English with limited strategies provided to make them more comprehensible for these students (Goldenberg, 2004). Knowing that ELL academic achievement rates tend to be lower than the rates of their peers is an area of great concern presented in the research.

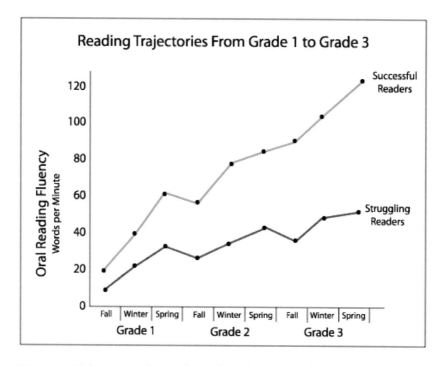

Figure 4: Primary reading trajectories without catch-up growth interventions.

Why Principal Leadership Matters

Researcher and Harvard Graduate School of Education Professor Richard Elmore stated in his book, *School Reform from the Inside Out,* "The purpose of leadership is the improvement of instructional practice and performance, regardless of the role" (2004).

The future for ELL students will be more challenging because of the lack of educational opportunities and the implications for the long-term impact to society if principal leadership at a school does not effectively close the achievement gap through effective interventions that allow for catch-up growth (Cooper, Chard, and Kiger, 2006).

According to Goldenberg (2004), reading teachers and content area teachers, as well as administrators at the district and building levels, are under intense pressure to not only understand the condition of our current educational systems, but to revamp existing instructional practice to improve the achievement levels of these students (Harvey, 2011).

However, it has taken until recently for research and leadership projects conducted between 2000 and 2010 by the Wallace Foundation to help with understanding of the "complexities of school leadership in new and meaningful ways" (Harvey, 2011).

What a difference that past decade has made in learning about the importance of effective principals having a school-wide learning goal for the academic success for all students as the focus of the school improvement plan (Knapp, Copland, Honig, Plecki, and Portin, 2010).

One of these key elements is the impact of the role of the principal and the work that he or she does to bring about second-order change in providing support to classroom teachers, create an appropriate school culture, leverage resources, and understand and implement valuable methodical, pedagogical, and adult learning strategies (Marzano, Waters, McNulty, 2005).

Researchers at the University of Minnesota and the University of Toronto reported an "empirical link between school leadership and improved student academic achievement" that has become a noteworthy finding from their major study over two separate six-year periods of time (Leithwood, et.al., 2010).

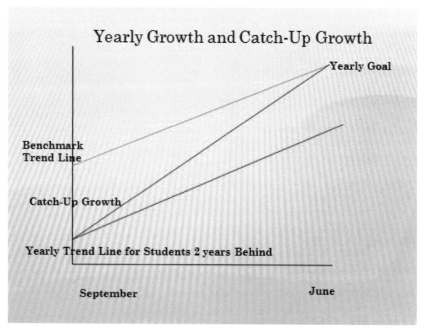

Figure 5: Catch-up growth: Key to closing the achievement gap.

Increasingly over the past two decades, when schools have been successful in closing the achievement gap for ELL students researchers have paid close attention to what kind of principal leadership occurred in each of the specific schools.

Researchers have concentrated on the role of the principal as the instructional leader in the school and the effect that role has in ensuring high academic success for diverse populations (Schlueter and Walker, 2008).

Schlueter and Walker's research indicates that the role of the principal can be indirectly correlated to the functioning of effective schools; nevertheless the research is inconclusive regarding the direct impact the principal may have on specific student achievement for second language learners.

Many current studies support the belief that the role of the principal does have an influence not only indirectly, but directly on the school's learning climate for all types of learners (Schlueter and Walker, 2008).

In the past decade, accountability from the federal level influenced second order change in schools. It is no longer tolerated by society as a whole to allow low-performing students to remain on the drop out trajectory. Aleman, Johnson, and Perez (2009) conducted a longitudinal study concerning the role of the principal and the effect on various student academic outcomes.

Studies indicate that the principal must thoroughly know how to teach Talented and Gifted (TAG) students and understand what must be done to provide an appropriate level of instruction for students on grade level and for those just slightly behind grade level standards.

Most critically, principals must be proficient in understanding what good instruction looks likes for the lowest performing, most intensive students and how to implement effective instructional strategies and programs systematically (Aleman et al., 2009).

In addition, other studies indicate that principals need to know how to create school improvement plans that will accelerate instruction for the most at risk of failing to graduate high school students, the majority of whom are ELLs, in order to close the achievement gap in the shortest amount of time possible (Heck and Hallinger, 2005).

The results showed that principals have a critical leadership role in ensuring that effective learning environments for all students are created and sustained (Aleman et al., 2009). Some of the most recent research shows that focused, caring leadership is the key to bringing change to multiple complex elements within a school's teaching and learning system (Aleman et al., 2009).

Researchers have reported that schools with similar resources and demographics may or may not produce the same kind of achievement for ELL students (Aleman et al., 2009). Aleman et al., in their work, found that schools that have been more successful in teaching large populations of ELLs have strong leadership that have focused goals and help their staff see the connections between these goals and student success. This involves the principal being effective in using data in daily conversations in order to bring life to teaching and learning goals

(Aleman et al., 2009). The principal utilized Professional Learning Communities and data teams to allow for structured collaboration in order to celebrate incremental student gains and system improvements in teaching and learning that can bring significant statistical results in student academic outcomes (Von Frank, 2009).

In addition to using data effectively, researchers agree that principals should also understand the importance of having high expectations for all students. In high performing schools with large percentages of ELLs, these student learn more as a result of more being taught to them to learn (Aleman et al., 2009). A positive outcome of strong principal leadership and positive ELL student academic performance may be in part due to the principal's ability to create a school culture of high expectations and student appreciation (Aleman et al., 2009).

In these schools, ELLs are expected to learn the same skills and concepts for each grade level and benchmark assessments are used to track and monitor deep mastery of skills. An instructional emphasis that provides students with a deep understanding of all concepts taught may have a positive correlation with student achievement scores.

Early analysis indicates the use of interventions such as re-teaching, scaffolding learning, tutoring, and after school instruction that are all planned through teacher collaboration appears to have a positive effect on students successfully learning to read by the end of grade three (Aleman et al., 2009; Baker, Gersten, Dimino, and

Griffiths, 2004; Linan-Thompson, Vaughn, Prater, and Cirino, 2006).

Research by Klingner and Artiles (2006) indicates that when ELLs are struggling to learn, read, and master math and content skills, then the teachers and principals who are most effective with these students are those who have an understanding of the differences between linguistic differences in their native language and in the second language that may be causing the student difficulties.

The intersection of literacy acquisition and language development is still being researched extensively, but given the persistent underachievement of ELLs, researchers agree that effective school leaders stay up to date with the most current scholarship available in order to advocate properly for ELLs (Goldstein, Fabiano, and Washington, 2005; Klingner and Artiles, 2006).

The question that researchers struggle with, however, is whether or not effective school leaders are keenly aware that when ELLs are achieving below their potential that it does not mean they automatically need to be referred for Special Education services. Studies report, in fact, that there is a disproportionate number of ELLs who have been inappropriately referred (Salend, Garrick Duhaney, and Montgomery, 2002).

Studies reflect a positive relationship between principal leadership and ELL student academic performance is a result of creating a culture of appreciation (Aleman et al., 2009). An atmosphere in a school that is not only positive, but is celebratory of diverse strengths is a characteristic of a school with large percentages of ELLs who are high performers.

The principal who lays the foundation for a positive culture where students and teachers alike feel respected, valued and appreciated will see positive results. When teachers feel supported and part of a team as teacher leaders and students and parents are part of a larger school community family, then there will be a true culture of appreciation (Aleman et al., 2009). This kind of family approach allows parental involvement programs to be more successful, especially if part of the program is orient parents to the U.S. school system as well as instruct them in how to help their child succeed in a caring, genuine manner (McElroy, 2005).

Key conclusions from recent research suggests three major points to consider when creating a foundation for improving education for ELLs (Goldenberg et al., 2005). Goldenberg concluded that teaching children to read in their native home language does promote reading achievement in English; what is known and proven about effective instruction in English holds true for instruction in Spanish and with ELLs; and it is the teacher's responsibility to make modifications to instruction for ELLs when they are being taught in English due to the students' language limitations (Goldenberg et al., 2005).

Similar to Goldenberg's first recommendation, most studies favor strong leaders who can advocate and ensure success for ELLs in their schools through the scheduling of native literacy and

English literacy programs. Researchers agree that it is the principal who is the one responsible for hiring the most qualified teachers who speak both English and Spanish at a high level.

In addition, the principal, as the instructional leader of the school, has the responsibility for completing frequent walk through observations of classroom instruction in order to provide feedback to teachers about specific instruction (Marzano et al., 2005). These observations ensure that the teachers hired are monitored and coached so that they are consistently teaching using the best practices in instruction (Kamps et al., 2007; Mathes, Pollard-Durodola, Cárdenas-Hagan, Linan-Thompson, and Vaughn, 2007; Mays, 2008; McDougall, 2010).

Theoretical Framework of the 21 Leadership Responsibilities

In 2003, the results of a meta-analysis that had been sanctioned by Mid-continent Research for Education and Learning (McREL) and conducted by Robert Marzano, Tim Waters, and Brian McNulty was released and validated decade old leadership theorists' ideas about the nature of principal leadership in schools. They gave educational leaders an important school leadership framework of The 21 Leadership Responsibilities of the School Leader, which outlines who is effective in bringing around first- and second-order change as result of their professional practices. This framework is referred to now as McREL's Balanced Leadership Framework (Waters, Marzano, and McNulty, 2003, see Appendix C).

This study reports that principals have an impact on student achievement. Although researchers agree that principals do, in fact, influence student academic outcomes for ELLs either indirectly or directly, the specific effect of a principal's role is partially undetermined and not completely clear at the present.

There is a need to research the knowledge taxonomy that has been applied to The 21 Leadership Responsibilities to see what principal characteristics are the most effective in supporting the learning for ELLs specifically.

The knowledge taxonomy organizes the list of 21 Leadership Responsibilities into four types of knowledge: experiential knowledge (knowing why this is important), declarative knowledge (knowing what to do), procedural knowledge (knowing how to do it), and contextual knowledge (knowing when to do it) (Waters, et. al, 2003).

Summary

This literature review provides a brief synopsis of the history of ELL student population growth, the ELL student achievement gap, and the role of leadership in schools to close the persistent achievement gap by creating school systems that can truly meet the academic needs of ELLs from Kindergarten through 12th grade.

Some contend that the principal leader has a strong indirect impact on student achievement, most notably at the elementary level, and identification of particular principal leadership characteristics promises to be the most effective way to improve outcomes for ELL students.

Early identification of these principal characteristics can assist current principals in their transformational efforts as well as be used to train new principals to be prepared for the task at hand in many of the nation's schools.

CHAPTER 3
METHODS

The purpose of this research was to explore, through the qualitative design of observation, recording, and interpreting the role of the principal in improving English Language Learner (ELL) outcomes in Spanish and Reading instruction and overall student achievement.

The perceptions of the principals of their behaviors as successful leaders in their respective schools were studied in order to uncover what traits or characteristics of good leadership looks like more specifically in schools with high ELL populations.

The researcher used the knowledge taxonomy developed by McREL as a framework to guide the development of the qualitative guide questions for the interview schedule to be used during the interviews.

The purpose for this design was to gather perceptions of principals and other emerging ideas during the interviews in order to detect prevailing patterns of principal behaviors and attitudes (Appendix B). The four areas of knowledge as described by McREL are experiential knowledge (knowing why this is important), declarative knowledge (knowing what to do), procedural knowledge (knowing how to do it), and contextual knowledge (knowing when to do it) (Waters, et. al, 2003). The researcher implemented research protocols applicable to the setting, principals, administrators, design of the research proposed, interview schedule, role of the researcher, and data analysis procedures in order to answer the research questions presented.

Specifically, order to provide an ethnographic research content analysis, the researcher used in-depth interviews with five former principals noting common patterns and themes discussed in all of the interviews. Each of the administrators selected participated in the SET-R (Systematic Explicit Teaching Routines) United States Department of Education grant research project with the University of Oregon during 2007-2011 school years. Each of these schools saw notable gains in student achievement in all subgroups of students in grades K-6.

Setting and Participants

Five elementary school administrators who were employed by the Hillsboro School District through school year 2010-2011 and currently live in the Portland Metro area are the individuals whose responses were analyzed for this study. The researcher contacted these individuals for a personal interview as a primary mode of data collection according to the limitations and delimitations presented earlier in this study.

The interviews were conducted in a school in Hillsboro, Oregon, after school was dismissed and students were no longer on campus. The interviews were private between the researcher and the participants and scheduled at a time most convenient for the interviewees.

Sampling Strategy and Rationale

The sampling strategy that was used is purposive sampling or typical case sampling technique because it is the most appropriate of the four types of techniques for nonprobability sampling for this particular exploratory study (Berg, 2009).

The researcher in this study selected the specific units of analysis to include samples that are the most useful for the purposes of this study and the student results of the SET-R grant.

Several principals who participated in the SET-R grant were not included as previously explained.

Research Ethics

The researcher adhered to George Fox University guidelines during the course of this research project in order to have a consistent research strategy and method for documenting this important phenomenon. The researcher obtained informed consent from each of the participants interviewed. Consent was obtained for use of data acquired from the tape recordings and journal notes used for analysis solely for the purposes of this particular study. A letter of consent was given to each participant describing the nature and purpose of this study (Appendix A). Confidentiality of individuals was carefully considered following the recommendations of George Fox University's Institutional Review Board (IRB) ethical policies and procedures. Each participant was issued a letter designation for the reporting of all data and analysis to reduce the risk of being identified. No research was conducted without the prior approval of the IRB.

In addition, data collected will continue to be securely stored on a secure server or in a locked file for up to three years, upon which time the researcher will take action to personally destroy the files. All study files, including participant consent forms, journal notes, interview recordings, site documents, student achievement data, and demographic data, will be destroyed by the researcher after the results have been written, disseminated, and the dissertation has been successfully completed.

Research Design

During this study the researcher took an insider's perspective as the author of this study (Neuman, 2007) by attempting to describe how the principals see the impact of their leadership abilities on ELLs through the process of observation, recording, and interpretation of perceptions from the interview transcripts.

The ethnographer's perspective was emic because the researcher is also a trained administrator employed as a principal within the same school district as those in the data set and will, as a result, attempt to understand and relate the principals' experiences and perceptions in a closer and more intimate portrayal.

The research process consisted of three general steps: contracting with the participants, the interview, and interpreting through narration of important observations by identifying noticeable concepts in order to draw reasonable conclusions. This interview and analysis process began in late December 2011 through February 2012 with final dissertation work completed during March 2012.

For the purposes of this study, the researcher created a base interview schedule of 15 open-ended questions and probes to be used within the format of the personal interview (Appendix B). The variety of the questions in the guide interview was designed to gather evidence on the educational background and training of the administrator as well as the perceptions and attitudes towards ELL students.

The guide questions addressed the principal's experience of improving student academic outcomes for ELLs and relationships with other administrators and teachers. Additionally, the guide questions address an evaluation of the aspects of the leading, teaching, and learning process for ELLs and major worries or complications encountered while being in the principal.

Interview participants were given the opportunity to add the future aspirations beyond retirement and any additional comments during the interview to capture all of the participants' perspectives of their work and leadership role.

The guide questions were developed through best practice research from principal leadership by using Marzano's work for McREL the list of The 21 Leadership Responsibilities.

The guide questions followed a series of three stages of personal interviewing: have the participants focus on their life history in light of the topic to the present, have the participants provide details of their experiences by reconstructing and relating important events and issues or opinions that surfaced, and then have participants reflect on the meaning of their experiences.

The researcher tied the experiences to the knowledge taxonomy framework from Marzano that was used to sort the 21 Leadership Responsibilities into four categories shared earlier.

The instrument was pilot tested by administering it to two other retired principals from HSD who were not part of the SET-R grant, but who had served in high poverty ELL schools. In addition, a graduate school colleague was given the interview and the feedback received from the three pilot interviews was used to revise the survey tool. Feedback from Dr. Shelton was also used for the revision work.

The researcher conducted semi-structured interview sessions informally at a location selected by the participant in order to have the flexibility to lead to relevant conversations as they arise during the one- to two-hour session. The researcher recorded written notes in a journal and recorded each interview session electronically using Audacity on her computer after obtaining permission from the participants. Electronic recordings of the interviews were transcribed.

The primary sources for this research were the transcriptions of the interviews and the journal notes. Member-checking was used to verify the accuracy of transcripts by emailing the completed transcripts to each participant for comments and feedback. All comments and feedback were included in the summary of the findings for each respondent. Peer-debriefing was completed by the researcher and the members of the research committee.

Data Collection and Analytical Procedures

According to Berg (2009), a researcher must choose some type of organized system in which information is coded. The researcher used the traditional coding procedures of working through the process of open coding, axial coding, and selective coding. This method is commonly used in qualitative research (Corbin and Strauss, 1990).

This researcher of this project analyzed data collected from the personal interviews conducted by the researcher by doing content analysis. Data collected includes school demographic data, site documents, journal notes, and transcriptions of recorded interviews. The researcher developed a coding strategy, as described below, to ascertain dominant themes that were shared with all participants in an attempt to employ the general process of analyzing qualitative data. The organization and interpretations of findings were based on this strategy.

After the interview text was carefully transcribed, the initial process of open coding was used with all interview transcripts. The researcher initially read them to identify key ideas or patterns that were sorted and coded into categories of response using NVIVO program to ease the work and save it electronically to avoid coding by hand using paper and pencil. However, hand coding was used eventually to sort and color code emerging patterns as the computer software became cumbersome to manage. Next, axial coding was used to separate principal responses. The researcher then began to narrow patterns to identify similar experiences in order to create a smaller number of categories and labels for study. The researcher incorporated the last step of the general process and procedures to analyze qualitative data of selective coding during the last phase of the interpretation using the coding process.

In applying open coding, the identified characteristics from various data sources were first listed. As part of the open coding process, important patterns in responses were noted. Next, in the axial coding stage, the researcher categorized data into tentative typologies. Typologies help to establish unique categories using common themes or leadership characteristics identified in the principal interviews (Bailey, 2007).

Finally, after further collapsing typologies, the final stage of selective coding assisted the researcher in looking for themes and noticeable patterns that described the specific leadership characteristics of principals at SET-R Program schools in the district.

Role of the Researcher

Over the course of this study, it was the primary responsibility of the researcher to adhere to all of the protocols and policies of the George Fox University IRB in a professional and an honorable manner. As a graduate student attempting to earn a doctoral degree through this research investigation, the researcher has a vested interest in pursuing this study through to a successful completion. The researcher is a professional educator and is currently an elementary school principal and responsible for the implementation of the Title IA, ID, and Title X of the consolidated ESEA federal grant for this Hillsboro School District.

The focus of this work through the researcher's professional job responsibilities is to continue to support the work for improving outcomes for disadvantaged youth and those most at-risk at not meeting state academic and graduation standards, specifically ELL students in the Hillsboro School District. Therefore, the researcher must have the ability to produce an objective and scholarly analysis independent of any district personnel or SET-R analysis, as clearly demonstrated in the final dissertation.

The researcher is committed to preserving the integrity of other district level administrators or researchers attempting to provide scholarly work on the same current issue and to carefully satisfy the committee requirements as requested.

Potential Contributions of the Research

The researcher's efforts are to explore conceptualized leadership traits or characteristics to more precisely identify which of McREL's 21 Leadership Responsibilities are most important to learn as a skilled principal for ELL students order to create greater understanding of where training modules need to be developed for new principal training or courses for Hillsboro School District. The training modules would first allow for training on all of the characteristics from McREL, secondly provide training on specific characteristics from this study that emerged as most effective for principals with schools with high ELL populations, and thirdly train the principals to be able to identify principles of effective reading/ language instruction in Spanish and English in the primary grades even if they do not speak Spanish.

Supporting principals in learning the differences and similarities between the Spanish and English orthographic systems well enough to articulate them and to leverage resources to make necessary instructional systematic changes would be part of the third module of professional development.

Addressing these areas specifically for Hillsboro's principals would most likely be a practical contribution to our district's current leadership practices, perceptions, and principal skill sets hopefully altering learning experiences of all students and ELLs in particular.

CHAPTER 4
FINDINGS

This study explored the role of principals in successfully improving English Language Learner (ELL) outcomes in their respective schools among a purposive sample of elementary principals who were employed by Hillsboro School District during the SET-R grant in the 2007-2011 school years.

The researcher was operating from a working hypothesis from the literature about what types of behaviors/ characteristics and principal experiences constitute creating school systems where ELLs are performing at high levels alongside their grade level peers. The researcher was attentive to operationalize the variables in an open-ended manner throughout the project.

Demographics of Hillsboro School District

According to the Hillsboro Chamber of Commerce, Hillsboro can be described as big town of over 200 square miles that has a little town feel or small-town charm. It is known for its high tech industry and Intel fabrication facilities throughout the city; nevertheless, farming and timber businesses remain an active part of the city. As one of Oregon's oldest communities within Washington County, Hillsboro has seen a huge growth in population in the past decade with many of those families being Hispanic (2011).

Hillsboro School District currently serves close to 21,000 students in programs offered in 35 elementary and secondary schools. Of those students, 53% are White, 33% are Hispanic, 7% are Asian/Pacific Islander, 3.3% are Multi-Ethnic, and 2.1% are Black according to the district's website (2012). Hillsboro's graduation rate of 91.5% surpasses the state average of 76.5%, however the district is focusing intensely on meeting the needs of all students, and especially ELLs were a persistent achievement gap remains in a dedicated pursuit of the District's mission to "Engage and challenge all learners to ensure academic success" (2011).

Demographics of Five Schools

An overview of each of the five schools using site documentation in order to obtain information creates context and enriches the final results. The overview includes demographic data, state student achievement data, and student performance results from OAKS (Oregon Assessment of Knowledge and Skills) tests. Data for this section was collected from Hillsboro School District website and from the Oregon Department of Education website. The percentage of students in grades 3-8 who either met or exceeded state standards or met their growth targets is used when reporting the federal rating.

School A had a student count of 446 students in May 2011. Of those students, 271 were Hispanic, 150 were White, 3 were American Indian/Alaskan Native, 10 were Asian/ Pacific Islander and 7 were African American. There were 81% of the students who were eligible for free or reduced lunches and 33.4% were ELL students. This school had an Oregon Report Card rating of *Satisfactory* and had a *Met* rating for the federal No Child Left Behind student achievement accountability requirements for Adequately Yearly Progress.

Student achievement data for OAKS for all students in Math was 72.5 % met or exceeded standards and 64.6 % of ELLs met or exceeded in 2010. Student achievement data for OAKS for all students in Reading was 87.7 % met or exceeded standards and 74.4 % of ELLs met or exceeded in 2010.

School B had a student count of 494 students in May 2011. Of those students, 371 were Hispanic, 129 were White, 4 were American Indian/Alaskan Native, 4 were Asian/ Pacific Islander and 6 were African American. There were 87% of the students who were eligible for free or reduced lunches, and 43.9% were ELL students. This school had an Oregon Report Card rating of *Satisfactory* and had a first year rating of *Did Not Meet* for the federal No Child Left Behind student achievement accountability requirements for Adequately Yearly Progress due to growth scores for special education subgroup.

Student achievement data for OAKS for all students in Math was 61.1 % met or exceeded standards and 48.5% of ELLs met or exceeded in 2010. Student achievement data for OAKS for all students in Reading was 87.6 % met or exceeded standards and 79.5 % of ELLs met or exceeded in 2010.

School C had a student count of 412 students in May 2011. Of those students, 394 were Hispanic, 82 were White, 4 were American Indian/Alaskan Native, 5 were Asian/ Pacific Islander and 7 were African American. There were 91% of the students who were eligible for free or reduced lunches and 57.5% were ELL students. This school had an Oregon Report Card rating of *Satisfactory* and had a *Met* rating for the federal No Child Left Behind student achievement accountability requirements for Adequately Yearly Progress.

Student achievement data for OAKS for all students in Math was 74.9 % met or exceeded standards and 68.8 % of ELLs met or exceeded in 2010. Student achievement data for OAKS for all students in Reading was 82.6 % met or exceeded standards and 77.5 % of ELLs met or exceeded in 2010.

School D had a student count of 458 students in May 2011. Of those students, 243 were Hispanic, 185 were White, 5 were American Indian/Alaskan Native, 34 were Asian/ Pacific Islander and 9 were African American. There were 58% of the students who were eligible for free or reduced lunches and 23.4% were ELL students. This school had an Oregon Report Card rating of *Satisfactory* and had a first year *Did Not Meet* rating for the federal No Child Left Behind student achievement accountability requirements for Adequately Yearly Progress due to growth scores in special education subgroup.

Student achievement data for OAKS for all students in Math was 77% met or exceeded standards and 71.8% of ELLs met or exceeded in 2010. Student achievement data for OAKS for all students in Reading was 94.3% met or exceeded standards and 89.7 % of ELLs met or exceeded in 2010.

School E had as a student count of 509 students in May 2011. Of those students, 320 were Hispanic, 156 were White, 4 were American Indian/Alaskan Native, 43 were Asian/ Pacific Islander and 7 were African American. There were 70% of the students who were eligible for free or reduced lunches and 35.8% were ELL students. This school had an Oregon Report Card rating of *Satisfactory* and had a *Met* rating for the federal No Child Left Behind student achievement accountability requirements for Adequately Yearly Progress.

Student achievement data for OAKS for all students in Math was 74.1% met or exceeded standards and 59% of ELLs met or exceeded in 2010. Student achievement data for OAKS for all students in Reading was 90.1% met or exceeded standards and 80% of ELLs met or exceeded in 2010.

Description of Participants

All of the professionals who participated in this research project were elementary school administrators at the time of their retirement in June 2011. All five individuals have a total of administrative and teaching experience ranging from 18 to 30 years. Two of the participants also worked as district-level administrators at some point during their career. One participant worked as a secondary vice principal at the high school level. Each of the participants were Caucasian females ranging from age 55-63. Each of these administrators were recognized by their colleagues for their expertise as principals and their work with ELLs. Two of the participants were nominees for the Hillsboro Chamber of Commerce Crystal Apple in Education Award and one participant was a Crystal Apple Award winner in 2011 during the last year of her principalship. The reputation of each of these five former administrators is recognized by their predecessors and colleagues. The good work that they did for students has become their legacy.

After retirement, two of the participants were hired by the Oregon Department of Education to work as mentor coaches for administrators in schools that have been identified as needing improvement because the two retired principals were from schools where students from all subgroups were succeeding at higher percentages than other schools.

Research Questions Findings

This study was guided by three research questions. The remainder of this chapter presents findings as a result of the research conducted. The three research questions are:

1. How do the principals promote or implement school culture expectations and best instructional practices in elementary schools with high populations of ELL students?

2. What level of general knowledge about leadership elements and characteristics do the principals possess whose students

performed well academically as measured by OAKS (Oregon Assessment of Knowledge and Skills test) in elementary schools with high populations of ELL students?

3. What do the principals regard as an effective approach or approaches to comprehensively serve ELL students in grades K-6?

The following sections of this chapter offer a discussion of the general findings associated with each of the three questions. The implications and conclusions of this research will be presented in Chapter 5.

Research Question #1.

How do the principals promote or implement school culture expectations and best instructional practices in elementary schools with high populations of ELL students?

The focus of research question one was on the procedural, contextual, declarative, and experiential knowledge base of effective school culture and best instructional practices among the principals for ELLs (Waters, et. al, 2003). The following paragraphs summarize the findings.

Participant A. This participant regards school culture as tied directly to the teacher and staff beliefs that all kids can really learn. She states that ELL students need to be held accountable for learning that occurs only after teachers have taught in a way that supports the needs of different language proficiencies (such as early intermediate level to the advanced level). Her response clearly shows that she had to deal with personnel issues related to staff not having high expectations or a belief that all kids can learn. She comments that initially this resistance impacted her work as a principal to move teachers to be willing to take the ELD (English Language Development) training as the initial step of implementation. She indicates that once necessary personnel changes were made the school culture shifted to a school-wide system that said, "Everyone's got language needs because of either being an ELL student or student in a high poverty school."

Participant A defines best practices in terms of the level of teacher engagement with the students, the learning process, and how well the students are engaged with the objective and purpose of each lesson. She states, "If students are not engaged... the learning is not going to happen." She regards engagement as an indicator of teacher effectiveness and understanding of best instructional practices. She states that on-going professional development using tools like *Teach Like a Champion* are important in changing instructional practices and school culture. This principal points out that school culture and best practices are, in her opinion, "interdependent and to be strived for in terms of excellence" and equity work.

Participant B. This principal defines school culture as a school that is positive and a place where adults are working together and always talking about teaching/learning and best practices. She believes that changing a school or district's culture is a process and takes a lot of additional learning specifically about second language learners for both the teachers and the principal. She points out that a principal has a key role in establishing an "ethic of care" and fostering school culture by having a genuine regard and respect for all people. Good school culture can be sensed immediately upon arrival in a school just like bad school culture can be easily picked up on by parents, students, staff, and other teachers from other schools. She reports that her school was able to change the way they were doing things to improve outcomes for ELLs and sees it as "an entire educational system change" for Oregon. However, she laments that she was at her last school only two years before retiring and states that knowing what she knows now would have a bigger impact on the work that she was trying to accomplish in her career prior to leading a school with a high ELL population.

Participant B states that in terms of best practices, school and classroom culture play a role in having the best instruction and student engagement that leads to student success. Additionally, she says that "the classroom has to feel safe and the kids have to understand, and the adults that work there as well, that it is okay to take risks." She states that the focus must constantly be on student learning with teachers having a "laser-like focus" to be strategic in their instruction each day. It is this kind of focus that provides students a learning opportunity to become literate in reading and writing and proficient in math by the end of elementary school. She states that students who are well prepared for middle school "have been given the keys to the kingdom."

Participant C. This participant believes that a positive school culture was part of the fabric of what she did as a professional to support students who were having difficulties through strong partnerships with the classroom teachers and the ESL department. She mentions that her whole staff recognized that they were teaching the students together and it was everyone's responsibility to learn the English Proficiency levels together. She says that the ESL teachers provided on-going professional development for the teachers and shared important teaching tools like sentence stems and frames that helped emphasize language goals. As a school the culture celebrated both English and Spanish languages as assets and some subjects were taught in Spanish, or a student's first language, so that students could attain the goal of learning the content without being held back by language development. She speculates that it was the strength of their school culture that allowed the staff at her school to implement school-wide ELD (English Language Development), implement content ELD in Math and Science by always trying to overlay language goals as an essential piece of instruction for ELLs. She indicates that their school culture encouraged students to feel safe enough to ask questions, feel welcomed, and recognized for their personal accomplishments.

Participant C emphasizes the importance of staff development and planning for effective instruction as the only way to ensure student success. She remarks that "being in the moment" with the student as the lesson morphs is the way the teacher monitors using check-ins or formative assessments are the best possible instructional practices for each and every lesson. She shares that nothing made her happier as a principal than "bell to bell instruction" with high expectations and student engagement. She agrees that school culture and best practices in instruction were related to one another.

Participant D. This participant started the answer to this interview question by telling a story about how the school where she was changed from grieving the lost monolingual learners to celebrating the emerging bilingual learners at their school as an example of how their school's culture drastically changed. This participant became aware of positive school culture that impacts ELLs by not allowing staff to say, "How are we going to teach those kids." Instead she modeled and expected a response that said, "What are we going to do for this child, that child, and the one over there?" By looking at children in this way, she believes that her school created a warm and caring culture that was focused on what the child could do in their native language and just how intelligent they really were. She reported that over time the staff began to make objectives clearer, used more visuals, taught with GLAD strategies, built systems that provided explicit vocabulary instruction, identified bilingual TAG students, and allowing monolingual students see how smart their bilingual peers really were helped to foster a positive culture for all students in her school. She also noted that school culture and best practices in instruction are tied together and that attitudes can change when students get good ELL instruction which strengthens the school culture around student expectations.

Participant E. This participant indicates that it took three years for the culture in her school to change from sending ELLs off to ESL classes with an expectation for them to be remediated to having a more "holistic" approach to having ELLs in their classroom getting support from both the ESL and classroom teachers in language instruction. She believes that the change of the culture had a huge impact on the teachers' abilities to teach more effectively using new best practices for ELLs that they understood that did lead to "significant improvement in our test scores."

This principal had previously worked at the district level as a Special Education Director and returned to the building level for the final decade of her career. She defines best practices in instruction as having various strategies that will work with different kinds of students that progressively get used as designed. She states that student engagement "is one of the most critical things you can do." She elaborates on the role of the principal in monitoring true student engagement in appropriate tasks related to the lesson objective. This principal also comments on how school cultures are very different and during the time she worked as a consultant she visited many buildings. After a while, she said she was able to easily determine what the school culture was in a building. They one thing that she says she could not fix as a principal was when teachers did not like kids. "If they like kids and care about them, then you have a place to start and that really build culture."

Each of the five participants agreed that school culture and a principal establishing an expectation for the use of best instructional practices were completely related. A positive school culture that reflects a positive vision that all students can learn regardless of their race, poverty, or any other potential barrier has to be established in order to ensure that teachers will use and implement best instructional practices such as establishing schoolwide ELD (English Language Development). This positive school or organizational culture, according to the participants, is also sensitive to the students' home culture, language, and honors each child's unique strengths. Principals who have a clear understanding of how to establish a positive culture by having a positive influence on teachers who in turn can positively influence students regardless of their personal culture is necessary, according to the participants.

Research Question #2

What level of general knowledge about leadership elements and characteristics do the principals possess whose students performed well academically as measured by OAKS (Oregon Assessment of Knowledge and Skills test) in elementary schools with high populations of ELL students?

The focus of research question number two was on the contextual, declarative, and experiential knowledge base of effective school culture and best instructional practices among the principals for ELLs (Waters, et. al, 2003). The following paragraphs summarize the findings.

Participant A. This participant started her response to discussing principal characteristics by stating that her current job working for Oregon Department of Education as a School Improvement Coach was all about "helping principals be effective leaders for school improvement." She is extremely knowledgeable about specific characteristics that principals need to possess to be effective change agents for all students, but specifically for ELLs. She reflects that one key area for a principal to understand is that many teachers do not understand or have not had experience with language proficiencies because they have not been trained as ESL specialists. Effective principals ensure their staff gets training in language instruction based on the levels of proficiencies to help them understand its importance in the context of their classroom. Additionally, this participant mentions that the principal must believe that all students are capable of learning and growing. The role of the principal is to provide opportunities for teachers to become more effective and part of a school culture that embraces the complexity of the work of school improvement. Moreover, she indicates that a strong characteristic of an effective leader of a school that is successful with ELLs is a principal who loves her job and has become an expert at hiring excellent teachers who have a belief in students' abilities, who are always willing to learn best practices, change instructional strategies and techniques based on student needs that shows in ongoing assessment, focus on equity issues, understand how to support and engage parents, and who are flexible enough to "improve their practice all the time relentlessly."

Participant B. Participant B defined the first principal necessary characteristic as the ability to know "a lot of stuff" specifically about first language acquisition, second language acquisition, and immigrant populations because these populations vary greatly from school to school. According to this participant, it is okay to not know it all when coming in, but an effective principal "gets busy to learn it by asking lots of questions" and learns to rely on other people who are the experts or specialists. She states that effective principals also expect their teachers to know about first and second language acquisition, where students are in their language development, and to know how to provide lessons that give students a chance to learn language by speaking, reading, and writing to grow them to the next language proficiency level. Additionally, effective principals are good observers and understand the systems in their buildings and how to make improvements or ongoing changes as necessary. She points out that effective principals for ELLs are good at data analysis, they know what is going on in the classrooms, and they communicate clearly to both students and parents about where the child is in his or her language development and academic progress. Participant B describes the most effective principals as those who understand how to help students access learning the language necessary to become successful in their second language (also known as L2 or Language 2) while preserving and growing in their native language (L1 or Language 1). This type of instructional model requires that the principal become a very good steward and advocate of resources such as time, money, and staff. Finally, Participant B believes that an effective leader needs to be open, full of positive energy, maintain a good perspective, and be willing to learn from everyone in the community while doing her part to "move all of us forward."

Participant C. Like several other interviewees, this participant reports that principals who are most effective with ELLs have "some basic knowledge about second language learners, the gifts they bring and the ways they need to be supported in schools." She shares that effective principals also have a real understanding about the "equity and inequity that exists" as well as the impact of the poverty issues. This participant emphasizes that the role of principals is to not only be knowledgeable themselves but to provide professional development for their teachers to gain basic skills about second language acquisition and how to best teach them at their various levels of learning and development. She agrees that the most effective instructional strategies and techniques for ELLs are good for all students and an important part of the school culture. "You know by golly they are effective strategies to use with all kids." This participant worked at the district level for a short time before returning to work as an elementary principal so that she could once again support students. Her experiences at the district level provide additional insight into necessary leadership characteristics; she believes that some of the necessary characteristics for principals to do well at the building level are also necessary in order to be an effective district-level Director, Executive Director, Assistant Superintendent, and Superintendent. Her experiences with various administrative positions were all interesting and challenging because they allowed her to "hone and improve" her skills such as facilitating changes, building capacity, and working with children and parents to build community. This participant said that even though working as an administrator is "very mentally and physically exhausting at times," it was really a job "that energized her," and that she looked forward to the start of each school year because it was a job she "really loved!"

Participant D. This participant identifies the ability to create and maintain strong interpersonal relationships as the primary characteristic of effective principals. This skill is important because it fosters strong professional teams "who know the child and what the child needs" specifically at their school. She states that these interpersonal relationships have to be built upon mutual respect, "respect for kids, and integrity." Additionally, effective principals model this respect for kids and her staff consistently by being "100% fair" and focused on the school's mission. She continues, saying that the characteristics she mentioned are "global characteristics" and that "modeling curiosity, monitoring student data, and a quest for knowledge about best practices, such as EBISS" (Effective Behavior Intervention Support Systems) is what effective principals do. Her job as a principal was to keep staff engaged in the change process, by which she means that good educators are always "trying to improve, as it is the nature of our business." She declared that it is not fair that mediocre teachers who are unwilling to improve are allowed to stay in the school system. Effective principals of ELL students expect a lot from themselves and their teachers, but know how to pace the training and implementation process at a level that teachers are not working at a frustration level given the urgency of the task at hand. She laments that being a principal now is more difficult than it has ever been and that principals need to be strong, resilient, and constantly learning along with their teachers. She is candid about this, saying:

> That comparing it [being a principal] to right now I feel like the plane is flying so high and so fast that everybody has to be able to everything while at the same time we are mantling and dismantling programs and there is no reflection time. It's just a tougher job, and now I think our district is telling us "you will do this." I support some of that because I have been again part of a collaborative team to work together to improve literacy instruction in Hillsboro. Together we worked smartly and efficiently that we weren't eight different wheels trying to invent in isolation. So the natural give and take of that created a lot of hugely successful systems in our district. In no way am I

criticizing my district at all, I am just saying that times are different now. The direction is, so intense now and the training required, the intellectual understanding of all of these programs at once, is tough to keep up with.

The changing landscape of accountability is changing the principal role at a drastic pace in Hillsboro, in Oregon, and across the nation.

Participant E. This participant mentioned that as a former principal of several high poverty schools with large ELL populations, she believes that the most "critical characteristic for principals ... is that you have to treat people with respect" and that effective principals have to "care about and enjoy working with kids." She says that there is an "obligation" on part of the teachers and principals to have a basic understanding of the "different cultural issues that are in play" for emerging bilinguals and just how complicated the learning process is for students learning multiple languages. She addressed the fact that teachers can "misunderstand the complexities of learning while learning a new language." Effective principals recognize that teachers have a need to learn some new technical skills to implement" well into their classroom instruction in order to make necessary changes to make sure all students are learning and progressing at an appropriate rate. She indicates that it is important for principals and teachers to realize there are misunderstandings about "where the kids are coming from, why they act the way they do, why they're not learning, or basic cultural differences." Lastly, she says that principals who handle the "managerial" parts of the job well ensure that they are able to keep those parts of the job from interfering from the "real leadership parts" such as hiring the most qualified teachers possible.

The participants all agreed that principals need to be aware of what professional development they need and their teachers need and to provide it in a timely manner with coaching support. Each participant referred back to experiences with implementing Systematic ELD (English Language Development). This professional development came as a result of assessing their need and the needs of their staff members to become more knowledgeable about second language acquisition. It was their strong sense of situational awareness that allowed them to gather the necessary clues about the overall health and well-being of their school that helped each participant become an effective change agent for ELL students. Collectively the participants agreed that it was because of the power of their relationships with the teachers and staff in their buildings that had the greatest impact on the success of their students and according to their perceptions the strength of their relationships as the principal could be used as a predictor of their ability to lead and manage the steps necessary for effective second order change.

Research Question #3
What do the principals regard as an effective approach or approaches to comprehensively serve ELL students in grades K-6?

The focus of research question number three was on the declarative and experiential knowledge base of effective school culture and best instructional practices among the principals for ELLs (Waters, et. al, 2003). The following paragraphs summarize the findings.

Participant A. This interviewee mentions that student achievement is linked directly to how effective a teacher is in monitoring students' needs and progress in order to "open pathways for them to achieve." The best principals understand the importance of having various processes like EBISS (Effective Behavior Intervention Support Systems) in place to "put a microscope" on students. Even though it is really hard work, it is an important approach. According to this participant, "We can unlock those doors, if we keep digging. It can be done for every student." In addition, this participant speaks positively about using ELD as an effective approach to comprehensively serve her ELL students. She describes how she worked closely with her leadership team and coach to get school-wide ELD into the master schedule so that "everybody was doing ELD" as a priority with high expectations. Her school completely moved from having a "pull out" model to a "push-in" model serving the needs of the students in the home classroom. Pull-out programs schedule daily lessons outside of the homeroom with a ESL teacher while push-in programs provide daily lessons taught by ESL teachers in a homeroom in collaboration with the regular education teacher. Teachers began to become "hypersensitive" to the needs of the

ELLs and started posting language objectives and providing systematic support. The whole goal of the ELD work was to get into the "consciousness of the teachers" and to get them to automatically provide language support throughout the day. Having every child get some kind of language support or enrichment based on proficiency levels was a way to really "turn a lot of kids around who had never been successful before." She shares that celebrating success is also an important approach and reflection of the expectation of excellence. Lastly, she mentions having after school programs as a way to give students extended time learning math, reading, and writing was as an approach that yielded good results for her ELL students in particular.

Participant B. Determining effective approaches to comprehensively serve ELLs was the focus of this participant's work at her last two schools. She mentions that it comes down to teachers and educational paraprofessionals being so invested in each student that they believe enthusiastically that the child can learn to a high level and are motivated to daily tell that child personally that she is smart, that she can do this, and that "I have never seen anyone do this just the way that you did it." Intimate contact in small groups with high engagement is a powerful approach to supporting ELLs. Having good communication with the students and high expectations is critically important to avoid "the soft bigotry of low expectations." The ongoing "Atta boy" is the only way to keep some students encouraged with the learning process as they master learning new content and a new language simultaneously. As a principal, this participant and her staff made an effort to let the students know that being bilingual is a gift and something positive to be celebrated. She describes the ELD program at her schools in this way:

> Students were being saturated all day long with language instruction and it is not a set aside subject. We are always learning language all day long. We are always working on it. It is not a surprise to see a language objective in Music. Everywhere we go is important. Really look at the individual…finding holes, filling holes one student at a time.

In addition, this participant shares another effective approach: use funds to support extended day learning programs with caring mentors during an after school program for ELLs based on a "hierarchy of need." Making opportunities such as after school programs, clubs, and the work with Right Brain Initiative available to ELLs created gains in test scores at the participant's two schools in a fairly short amount of time. An important part of making the after school approach successful for students is to bring in role models and mentors who have had to travel a similar road so that they can speak to the possibilities with the students and validate that it might be really hard, but that the students can do it. Not allowing the students think they can't do it or they shouldn't even try is such a simple, but necessary approach and one approach that had the most impact on her students, according to this interviewee.

Participant C. This participant, like her colleagues, mentions that the most effective approach in serving ELLs comprehensively is having extremely skilled, knowledgeable, and dedicated teachers who believe that it is "possible to help all children grow in their achievement." Other than the student's parent, the participant emphasizes that the teacher is the most powerful influence and can make a "tremendous difference in the lives of children and how they achieve."

Having the best trained teachers is so powerful especially when they are "committed to ELD (English Language Development) instruction as a whole school. The approach used in the participant's last school was to have all teachers "up to speed" with ELD strategies such as language forms and functions so that language was being taught throughout the day and not just by the ESL teacher. The classroom teachers took the lead with ELD instruction and as a school everyone was really strategic about language instruction. According to the participant, this turned out to be the most effective approach that helped move her school out of AYP sanctions within less than a two year period. She happily pointed out that these results had a profound effect on their community and school. "The neat thing was that kids felt successful, teachers felt successful, and parents felt much more positive about the direction we were going."

In addition to having effective teachers implementing ELD well, this participant agrees that having different "elements" in a school like extended day programs, small group instruction, and different curriculum were approaches that she used and saw noteworthy results for her ELL students.

Participant D. This participant started out by saying that the most effective approach to comprehensively serving ELL students is to ensure that the teachers, staff and principal work together as a team in a reflective manner by using "objective hard data" to measure what was going on for students. The school professionals must be willing to change instructional practices to best meet student needs by providing "seamless experiences" from grade to grade within a school. The professional development from the district was key in getting data teams in place and functionally well within each of the schools, she says.

> Teachers learned how to sit and talk about data on their own and use their own assessments to plan for their curriculum. That became systematized in our district through EBISS and that took us to another level... because they were not waiting on me (the principal) to drag them through a pile of data.

She describes how teachers raised expectations when they saw their struggling students begin to master concepts that were not mastered before based on changes made as a result of data teams. "There was not more let's hope by June they got it. We know right now they got it... knowing our kids are smart was profoundly huge in terms of getting results." Additionally, she says that the approach of using data teams to change instructional practices changed student outcomes that lead to higher expectations, celebrations of student successes and changed attitudes on the part of the teachers and staff. She regards her ESL team as key to supporting the work and important leadership in having effective data teams as an approach to serving ELL students well.

Another approach used by this participant was to be aggressive in identifying all of the TAG (Talented and Gifted) students in her schools that reflected the demographics specifically. She clearly appreciates the work of school professionals when she shares that her specialists and classroom teachers worked tirelessly to determine students' strengths by "digging deeply to figure out what was going on" and to make sure each student was given the best and most appropriate instruction possible. Her last school became a model for her school district in how to best identify Latino students for TAG.

This participant indicates that the principal, teachers, and staff in a school must be willing to have a "whatever it takes attitude" as an approach to working towards finding solutions and putting the best possible instructional program in place for ELLs. This means that everyone must be willing to work long hours and "if you don't feel that you are trying to do some magic, then you are in the wrong job." This approach can only be effective for ELLs and other students if the principal is able to hire "well," which is often indicated by those teachers who are willing to work long hours as demonstrated by those who are willing to take the work home with them on the weekend, have a strong commitment to their work, bring in high energy, communicate authentically with students and parents, and are always looking for ways to improve their teaching ability.

Participant E. This participant says "I really do believe that all students can learn," which is how she describes effective approaches to serving ELLs. She says that having a committed principal, highly trained teachers, and knowledgeable staff are crucial components to having an effective approach as a school team. Teacher training in the area of ELL populations and poverty student strengths, needs, and best instructional practices is another effective approach that served her students well in two schools. She explains her role in helping the teachers really take ownership of that achievement data.

> I think it was critical that we helped the teachers get over that obstacle of not understanding that they were responsible for what was going on in their own classroom and not feeling defensive about that, just being able to share the data and not make excuses for the data, but to look at it objectively.

This approach of having teachers technically trained was part of a school-wide three year plan. The focus of that plan was to have teachers take ownership of their students, monitor learning and "be aware of where students were on their achievement cycles," and to establish collaboration between the staff, teachers, and specialists for ESL, Special Education, and Title I. Student gains at the end of the three years indicated that their plan was successful in improving outcomes for ELL students. In conclusion, the discussion of the results from the interviews indicated several specific principal leadership characteristics and necessary for creating school systems where ELLs are performing at high levels alongside their grade level peers.

A reoccurring response from the participants in regards to what they perceived as an effective approach to comprehensively serve ELL students was the implementation of Systematic ELD and the posting and referencing of Language Objectives alongside all other teaching objectives. Each participant invested plenty of time, money, and coaching for teachers to be sure that ELD was implemented well to ensure sustainability. Another approach the participants agreed was effective was to change the kind of instruction being offered to students in extended day programs both in an after school and summer format. Lastly, using the power of relationships and teacher collaboration to drastically change the current ESL teaching model was mentioned by many of the participants as an effective approach.

This model change moves from one model where students are pulled out of their classroom instruction for remediation with the ESL teacher away from their classroom teacher and peers to having the ESL teacher push into the classroom to assist their classroom teacher with scaffolding the instruction to meet the language needs of ELL students.

From their experience, the principals agreed that having the ESL teacher push into the students' classrooms is ideal.

CHAPTER 5
ANALYSIS, DISCUSSION, AND
CONCLUSIONS

This qualitative study was designed to develop a more comprehensive understanding of the role of the principal in successfully improving English Language Learner (ELL) educational outcomes in their high poverty, Title I schools.

The participants who were interviewed were limited to a purposive sample of elementary principals who were employed by Hillsboro School District during the SET-R grant from school years 2007-2010. Personal interviews were used to examine whether or not specific principal behaviors and leadership characteristics have an effect on ELL educational outcomes and which of The 21 Leadership Responsibilities related to positive ELL achievement results based on the perceptions of each of the veteran principals.

In Chapter 2, a review of the literature was previously presented that now will be linked to the findings from this research study. By comparing the five principals' comments and perceptions of leadership characteristics/traits and principal behaviors, an analysis will be presented in this chapter that link up the characteristics into one of the four knowledge categories of the guiding framework in order to answer the three research questions.

The three research questions that were developed from the

working hypothesis or guiding framework of Marzano, Waters, and McNulty's list of The 21 Leadership Responsibilities for this study will be used to closely examine and categorize the participants' answers into one of the four knowledge categories of experiential, declarative, procedural, and contextual knowledge order to interpret what might have occurred in the schools where the principals were leaders and the ELL students were making significant gains in student achievement (Waters et al. 2003).

First, how do the principals promote or implement school culture expectations and best instructional practices in schools with high populations of ELL students?

Second, what level of general knowledge about leadership elements and characteristics do the principals possess whose students performed well academically as measured by OAKS (Oregon Assessment of Knowledge and Skills test) in schools with high populations of ELL students?

Third, what do the principals regard as an effective approach or approaches to comprehensively serve ELL students in grades K-6?

Leadership does matter and two principals in particular at Thomas Edison Elementary and Signal Hill Elementary in Long Beach, California have used their roles to drastically impact the outcomes for the ELLs in their schools. These administrators won the National Center for Urban School Transformation (NCUST) award in 2008 for Excellence in Urban Education. These two schools, along with two others from Florida and Texas, are successfully closing the achievement gap.

Hillsboro has several great schools like Edison and Signal Hill in Long Beach, California with former, seasoned leaders who may be able to shed some light on ways of knowing how to set in motion the most effective second order change necessary for ELL success. This research could offer some insight regarding how specific principal behaviors possibility listed on McREL's balanced leadership for areas of knowledge framework could be used to support leaders of schools with high ELL populations and less of Karr's work as originally proposed as it is more focused on English Language Development instruction for teachers and not focused on principal leadership.

Analysis and Discussion

Research Question #1: How do the principals promote or implement school culture expectations and best instructional practices in elementary schools with high populations of ELL students?

All of the principals were queried about their leadership experiences in promoting school culture expectations and best instructional practices. All five of the participants interviewed stated that the way principals promote or implement school culture expectations and best instructional practices for ELLs was through having a clear understanding regarding what is required to establish positive school culture and set expectations for best instructional practices in their schools making these a reality as a result of principal actions.

According to Hanson "every school has a culture" (2001). Culture is both explicit and implicit and is shared as a result of the beliefs, values, and feelings from each of the individuals working at a school, making the culture unique because each school setting is made up unique students and teachers. Even though it is not visible the school's symbols, mission statement, use of resources, and celebrations communicate what is of particular importance to everyone in the school.

Marzano, Waters, and McNulty (2005) assert that leaders who are effective at establishing positive school culture have a positive influence on teachers who then have a positive influence on students. Principals work through teachers, staff, and parents to create a positive culture or a true ethic of care and respect that becomes the primary way that leaders can bring about change for students (Leithwood and Riehl, 2003).

The responsibility of establishing positive school culture is fifth on the list of The 21 Leadership Responsibilities and the behaviors associated with this responsibility promote cohesion, well-being, purpose, and a shared vision among staff (Marzano et al., 2005). Each of the five principals were articulate about each of these areas related to establishing positive school culture and added that only within a positive school culture can a principal set high expectations related to use of best practice instructional techniques and high expectations as critically important to avoid "the soft bigotry of low expectations" as Participant B stated passionately. Sergiovanni (2004) refers to this kind of culture as a "community of hope."

Four of the five participants said that both school culture and best practices were related to one another. Participant D commented that shifting a school's culture to one that values both Spanish and English literacy was an obligation and foundational to ensuring outcomes that are equitable for all students regardless of their race, gender, or social economic status.

Instead of allowing the teachers to say, "How are we going to teach those children with a different language," a principal should ask, "What are we going to do for this child, that child, and the one over there?" This was a question she expected her teachers to take seriously and answer with their actions and changed instructional approaches such as using more visuals and providing explicit vocabulary instruction. It was not long, she said, that the entire was focused on "what the child could do in their native language and realized just how intelligent they really were."

Generally all of the participants agreed that establishing a positive culture and expecting best practices in instruction is a result of a principal knowing why it is important (experiential knowledge), what (declarative knowledge) and how (procedural knowledge) to do what needs to be done for students, and when (contextual knowledge).

One participant stated that it is okay not to know, but that a "principal needs to get busy and learn it." Fullan (2001) suggests that principals have an important day-to-day responsibility of knowing effective best practices in curriculum, instruction, and assessment in order to set the expectations that best practices will be used throughout the school.

Principals must develop a broad knowledge base to stay current with is happening in the classroom and in research and as one participant emphasized "pace the work" for the staff over a set period of time.

Marzano (2005) adds that reading books, attending district professional development courses, attending graduate courses, or attending conferences are behaviors principals can engage in to gain extensive knowledge about effective instructional, assessment, and classroom practices as part of carrying out Instructional Leadership, the thirteenth responsibility.

Most of the participants attested that school culture expectations and best practices in instruction are considered specific actions that a principal can take towards improving student achievement.

Wimpleberg, Teddlie, and Stringfield (1989) posit that defining specific actions to take as a principal is an important step in moving from principal leadership operating only at a general level with a focus on general characteristics like establishing a vision for the school to taking actions that will impact students.

Moreover, all of the interviewees concluded that all ELL

students and students in high poverty schools need to have a shift to a school-wide instructional system that supports the language needs of all students through English language development instructional strategies where their native language is valued and appreciated as part of their school culture and students are given opportunities to learn a new language while retaining their native language.

Susana Dutro (2009) confirmed that developing a student's second language while continuing to teach content in their native language towards bilingualism has proven to be a current advancement in programming models for ELLs. All of the participants agreed that ELD (English Language Development) was a powerful instructional strategy that advanced student achievement and changed the culture of their schools.

The participants' definition of having a positive school culture that is respectful of different languages is concurrent with researchers who state that this leads to long term successful outcomes for ELL students along with a strong instructional leader (Dutro and Helman, 2009). A positive school culture that reflects a positive vision that all students can learn regardless of their race, poverty, or any other potential barrier has to be established in order to ensure that teachers will use and implement best instructional practices such as establishing schoolwide ELD (English Language Development). This positive school or organizational culture, according to the participants, is also sensitive to the students' home culture, language, and honors each child's unique strengths.

Principals who have a clear understanding of how to establish a positive culture by having a positive influence on teachers who in turn can positively influence students regardless of their personal culture is necessary, according to the participants.

Research Question #2: What level of general knowledge about leadership elements and characteristics do the principals possess whose students performed well academically as measured by OAKS (Oregon Assessment of Knowledge and Skills test) in elementary schools with high populations of ELL students?

All five of the participants interviewed had previous leadership training through undergraduate and graduate course work, state and district training courses, and on the job training and mentoring by coaches and specialists about what leadership characteristics principals need to possess to be an effective leader for ELL students.

All of the five participants agreed that principals must have a clear understanding of three of the four areas of the McREL framework of contextual knowledge (when to do it), declarative knowledge (what to do), and experiential knowledge (why it is important) in relation to the overall characteristics. The how to do it or procedural knowledge is the responsibility of the teachers when it comes to directly instructing the students using specific methods and is not as critical for the principal to understand at a methodical level for each grade level and language proficiency level. Four of the five principals mentioned that it was the district-sponsored training in the recent past that was most beneficial to their learning and gave the example of Dutro's ELD training as the most impactful.

All of the participants agreed that the leadership characteristics they thought were beneficial to their work with ELLs during the SET-R grant and beyond related to principals' need to understand what the "teachers do not understand about teaching, learning, and why the students may be having difficulties" currently in their school. The eleventh characteristic from McREL's list is called Intellectual Stimulation. Marzano, Waters, and McNulty (2005) affirm that intellectual stimulation refers to the effort made by the principal to provide ongoing training to teachers and staff to keep them aware of the recent educational theories and practices and to establish "meaningful dialogue regarding research and theory" (Supovitz, 2002).

The participants agree with researchers who maintain teachers of ELLs need to be allowed to learn how to better serve their students through coaching by providing clear learning objectives, analyzing data, and having a basic understanding of second language acquisition along with the stages of student development through the process is important in improving outcomes (Goldenberg, 2008). Knowledge is built, shared, created, and managed in terms of student needs, according to Fullan's (2001) description. One of the participants said, "Effective principals realize teachers have an obligation to have a basic understanding of the different cultural issues that are in play for emerging bilinguals and how complicated the learning process is for students learning multiple languages." All of the principals agreed with Dutro's English Language Development work to provide daily instruction in language acquisition (Dutro, 2009).

A common thread throughout the interviews was the importance of interpersonal relationships as foundational to all facets of the work that needs to be done ensure student success. Waters et al. (2005) agree that almost all researchers who have explored leadership characteristics refer to establishing healthy working relationships is "central to the effective execution" of good leadership.

The characteristic of Relationships is listed as number eighteen on the list of The 21 Leadership Responsibilities and is defined as the awareness that a leader has in the personal lives of each of the teachers and staff in their school (Waters et al., 2005).

These relationships need to be genuine through face-to-face experiences according to Richard Elmore (2000). Fullan (2001) indicates it is the strong emotional bonds that are created by the principal with the teachers and staff that keep everyone focused and together during times of confusion or uncertainty.

Most of the participants commented that the strength of these relationships is a reflection on the principal's ability to hire excellent teachers and then, because of strong relationships, retain those teachers at their school. Strong relationships also encourage school personnel to work to the best of their abilities in strong professional teams "who know each child and what each child needs to succeed."

The two interviewees who had worked outside of the elementary level mentioned the power of relationships in their work as a high school guidance counselor and a social worker. They emphasized that often it is the relationships that are created with the staff, students, and parents that can carry the work over the long haul despite the many challenges or setbacks because of a strong and committed community.

Generally all of the interviewees agreed that in addition to having strong interpersonal relationships and the ability to be intellectually stimulating, effective principals need to possess a strong sense of situational awareness of what is going on in their school, the classrooms, and with the community in relation to serving the needs of the students. Waters et al. (2005) stated that situational awareness is the awareness that the leader has about the "details and undercurrents regarding the functioning of the school and the use of this information to address current and potential problems."

Moreover, Lashway (2001) cautions the principal to distance ego from the events of each day in order to assess the overall health and well-being of the organization in order to gather clues about what new may be coming as an opportunity or as a concern.

Research Question #3: What do the principals regard as an effective approach or approaches to comprehensively serve ELL students in grades K-6?

All five of the principals were queried about their perceptions and their declarative knowledge (what to do) and experiential (why it is important) knowledge of what approaches were necessary in order to serve ELLs comprehensively.

In addition to providing systematic English Language Development (ELD) instruction daily as a consistent theme across all five interviews, three of the five principals referred to the importance of establishing after school programs and extended year opportunities as ways to be innovative about meeting the needs of ELLs. Participant A mentioned, "We can unlock those doors, if we keep digging. It can be done for every student. We can open pathways for them to achieve." McREL suggests the Change Agent as the second characteristic and it is defined as the principal's ability to "temporarily upset the school's equilibrium" in order to meet student needs in ways that have not been done previously.

Silins, Mulford, and Zarins (2002) posit that effective change agents are the leaders who are protective of teachers, those who are taking risks and doing new things for students to improve outcomes. The principal empowers the teachers to do what is needed for each child, including establishing quality after school and extended day learning programs.

Three of the principals mentioned that after school programs or summer programs were not new to their schools, but changing the format and expectations for after school to be an extension of the day's learning versus a play time or babysitting brought results for ELLs. The participants agree with Waters et al. (2005) that the Change Agent needs to be the one who consider new and better ways of doing things and to consistently attempt to "operate at the edge versus the center of the school's competence.

The last approach is to change the ESL model from a pull out model of service to a push in model where all the students' needs in the homeroom are served through collaboration of the classroom teacher and ESL specialist working together. This important approach was initially implemented in all five of the elementary schools as a result of the principal inspiring the "teachers to accomplish things that might have been out of their grasp" and by being a driving force behind the ELD initiative and ESL model changes.

Kaagan and Markle (1993) theorize that the positive emotional tone of the principal allows for an environment that abounds with innovation and new ideas. The participants agree that along with this innovation comes a willingness to learn and make changes because the teachers are "hypersensitive to the needs of ELLs." They are willing to post language objectives, provide systematic support, change program models, and offer additional learning periods according to one of the principals whose school went out of sanctions as a result of this type of work.

Waters et al. (2005) define this leadership characteristic as the Optimizer, a principal who sets an emotional tone in a school that optimism and energy about initiatives and portrays a positive attitude about the ability of the staff to accomplish "substantial change."

Only one of the principals had secondary experience and she lamented that at high school change is more difficult because the tone is not always as positive or supportive. Another principal who had been in education for the past thirty-five years lamented that the role of the principal to set a positive tone has become more and more difficult, especially in the last decade, due to increasing pressures and significant cuts in resources.

Implications for Educational Leaders

First, it was not surprising to discover that three of the major characteristics that emerged as themes from the interviews were listed as part of the necessary seven of The 21 Leadership Responsibilities for second-order change according to Marzano, Waters, and McNulty (2005).

The responsibilities discussed by the principals as most important in being an effective principal for ELLs were Culture, Instructional Leadership, Intellectual Stimulation, Change Agent, and Relationships. The three matching themes from the interview responses presented in the previous discussion are underlined on the list below and the two themes that are similar to the interview responses are presented on the list in italics.

The McREL list of these responsibilities is in rank order of importance in relation to second-order change.

1. *Knowledge of Curriculum, Instruction, and Assessment*
2. Optimizer
3. Intellectual Stimulation
4. Change Agent
5. Monitoring/Evaluating
6. Flexibility
7. *Ideals/Beliefs*

The priorities for a principal seeking to lead a school that will have successful student outcomes will need to embrace the corresponding characteristics and take appropriate actions for each of the characteristics described for Optimizer, Intellectual Stimulation, and Change Agent (Waters et al., 2005).

Participants in this study agree that leading in a positive way, as a driving force behind the change with high expectations that staff members can do the necessary work to improve ELL outcomes, is acting as an Optimizer. Leading staff in trainings and discussions about recent research and ongoing best practices for second language acquisition and native language instruction is an example of providing Intellectual Stimulation specific to the needs of ELLs. Communicating well with the teaching staff in a Hillsboro school specifically will lead to unique change in the District. An unbridled willingness as a leader to take risks on cutting edge, best practices strategies without any guarantees to make improvement for ELLs is the function of a Change Agent. Logically, it would seem that the first three characteristics that overlapped with the McREL list would be the most necessary for a principal to be truly effective.

Comparison of Second Order Change Leadership Responsibilities	
List of 7 Responsibilities (Marzano, 2005)	List of 6 Responsibilities (Petersen, 2012)
1. Knowledge of Curriculum, Instruction, and Assessment	1. Knowledge of Second Language Acquisition
2. Optimizer	2. Optimizer
3. Intellectual Stimulation	3. Intellectual Stimulation
4. Change Agent	4. Change Agent
5. Monitoring/Evaluating	
6. Flexibility	
7. Ideals/ Beliefs	5. Organization and Student Culture
	6. Relationships with Teachers and Students

Figure 6: Comparison of second-order change between Marzano (2005) and Petersen (2012).

Next, the results of this study show two characteristics that were similar to the list for second-order change even though they were not an exact match (Waters et al., 2005). Culture was discussed extensively and although it is not one of the seven listed by Marzano et al. (2005), it is related to the last characteristic of Ideals/Beliefs. The importance of operating with consistent ideas and beliefs and establishing a culture based on those ideas and beliefs are interrelated. Culture and establishing a positive culture where all students are expected to learn was reoccurring theme across each of the five interviews.

The underlining understanding that all students are respected and expected to learn was tied closely to the relationships that principals had with all members of their school community. Instructional Leadership was identified by the participants and it closely resembles Knowledge of Curriculum, Instruction, and Assessment, the number one characteristic for second-order change; thus, the ability to lead innovation is necessary as indicated by this study.

The last characteristic that emerged from the study, Relationships, does not relate at all to one of the seven important second-order change characteristics according to McREL. This was a real surprise to me that relationships were not listed by McREL for second order change, but I was not surprised it was mentioned by the principals knowing how close each one was to their teachers, staff, students, and families.

I heard each of the participants mention the power of relationships as the fuel to do the hard work many times during the interviews and in the cross walk between the interviews. Findings from this study conclude that relationships are foundational to innovating change for ELLs, but according to Marzano, Waters, and McNulty (2005), relationships are only necessary in the day-to-day management of schools.

The researcher's personal experience as a district level and building level administrator attests to the fact that relationships are necessary in order to begin the work of second-order change for ELL students. Positive relationships allow the school leaders to gain the trust of the teachers, staff, and parents in the ELL community so that those relationships hold the vision of the common work and goals together during the challenges of implementation over a several year period.

Contrary to the findings presented by McREL, the results of this study indicate that there may be some additional characteristics for principals to study that are related to second-order change for ELL students.

Fred Luthens (1988) in his study on the difference between successful leaders, those who have been promoted quickly, and effective leaders, those with high performing units of responsibility along with committed and satisfied employees, points out that the key is understanding what effective leaders are doing in their day-to-day activities as compared to the activities of successful leaders.

Effective and successful school leaders are not politically

motivated, but in their day-to-day work attend to the human-orientated activities that require excellent interpersonal relationship skills to empower subordinates in a way that is satisfying while the person is working towards the goal of the organization. Luthens' work on effective managers ties closely to the results of this study, indicating that one of the six necessary responsibilities of a principal to bring second-order change is to be relational.

The third implication for educational leaders is the conclusion that the leadership training for elementary and secondary principals is similar because it is based on state proficiency requirements and yet the testing results for students in the elementary levels are consistently higher for Native Spanish Speaking students than those in middle and high school in Hillsboro where the achievement gap still exists to a greater degree.

The researcher pondered the problem of why positive gains for ELLs can be made on the student trajectories at the elementary level and then lost at the secondary level. This query would be a good basis for future research projects looking specifically at instructional strategy differences between elementary and secondary and the overall demand of grade level standards as students' progress towards graduation.

Appendix D shows the six responsibilities as molecules representing the chemistry that an effective principal needs to possess as a result of this study. The two responsibilities that are the outside circles of the diagram that hold the other four responsibilities together are Organizational and Student Culture and Teacher and Student Relationships. These two are the epoxy that holds the rest of the molecule together that contains the remaining four traits of Intellectual Stimulation, Change Agent, Knowledge of Second Language Acquisition, and Optimizer.

Learning from the interviews of five former Hillsboro principals, the next best step for school districts is to train all current leaders on the 21 Leadership Responsibilities as the framework that defines prerequisites of a leader. This can occur through the Principal Professional Learning Communities (PLC) training structure to train principals on the seven responsibilities necessary for second order change according Marzano, along with the results from this study identifying the six responsibilities identified as necessary for being an effective principal in a school with high ELL populations (see Appendix D).

Lastly, providing ongoing coaching support for principals would facilitate a faster learning curve for all principals new to working with schools with high ELL populations to become proficient with the six leadership responsibilities instead of being left on their own to try to figure things out, a method that, according to the interviews, resulted in many years of diminished success with ELL students.

Our students deserve better than individual principals trying to figure things out for them in isolation. Coaching towards common expectations and goals systematically could potentially lead to the desired change necessary for closing the achievement gap for ELLs (see Appendix E).

Recommendations for Future Research

Based on this research project, second-order change initiatives in Hillsboro School District have been implanted in the past have been implemented with extensive professional development for teachers on the specifics of the strategies such as English Language Development or Houghton Mifflin instruction. However, both elementary and secondary principals have received little professional development in effective leadership responsibilities simultaneously to lead the work as the teachers received training.

It was apparent that the five elementary principals who were interviewed had to "build the airplane while they fly it," as one mentioned, by relying on each other for help, being willing and having the ability to learn quickly, and by attending graduate courses. In 2011, the Hillsboro School District reconfigured its administrative support network due to budget constraints. The district moved from four executive directors overseeing the work of each of the four feeder groups that lined up with Hillsboro's four high schools to only two executive directors, one for elementary and one for secondary, each responsible for supporting principal leadership work through a highly defined Professional Learning Community (DuFour, 2004) model.

It appears that more research of this kind is necessary for the principals at the secondary levels in schools with successful ELL achievement to determine which of The 21 Leadership Responsibilities would be most beneficial for their use since the results of this study were based on experiences of elementary principals. It would be fascinating to see how their lists of responsibilities might compare to the list from the elementary principals who were interviewed.

Budget restraints and limited professional development funding from federal supplemental grants and the lack of coaching support to guide administrators through challenging leadership issues is a noticeable issue for the participants of this study.

Additional scholarly investigation is necessary in order to provide realistic professional development options regarding how to support "doing the right work" of training and coaching principals in making good decisions about "what to work on" (Elmore, 2003) in Hillsboro School District.

The query about secondary leadership characteristics in Hillsboro could be a good basis for future research projects looking specifically at instructional strategy differences between elementary and secondary levels as a possible reason for why gains made in the elementary grades cannot be sustained in secondary.

Studying current student instructional profiling practices and data team protocols for appropriate placement into core, supplemental, and or intervention programs as recommended as part of the tiered method recommended by Response to

Intervention could be beneficial and insightful in regards to the overall demand of grade level standards and lack of access to instruction aligned with these standards as students' progress towards graduation.

It may be that the instructional strategies presently used focus only on meeting minimum acceptable English reading skills while depriving the student access to content rich, rigorous instruction necessary to perform well in classes necessary for graduation.

In conclusion, professional development training for principals on specific leadership responsibilities that impact second-order change to impact ELL students is a best practice that needs to be considered by school districts, including Hillsboro School District.

It is apparent that the past model of limited training and/ or principals learning characteristics while simultaneously learning their jobs is an ongoing challenge that has caused conflict and confusion for a few schools with high numbers of ELLs who are not performing well on achievement measures.

Marzano, Waters, and McNulty posit that implementation of successful second-order change requires a school leader to "ratchet up" his drive, passion, and optimistic attitude as the work of deep level change "takes a personal toll on a school leader and might explain why many promising practices have been abandoned" (2005).

An extensive training and coaching plan for principals is imperative for Hillsboro to be successful in closing the achievement gap for ELL students. Developing training to teach each of the five areas identified in Appendix D would be a probable starting point for my district to begin in supporting our building principals as they take on the task of leading second order change initiatives in each of their buildings.

The role of district level leadership is to filter through educational theory and to be truly wise consumers of theory in order to put it into practice soon enough to bring about necessary change to impact students to the fullest degree.

What I have learned from this study from the experience of these successful principals may be a starting place for training other principals to help our District move from having a few schools doing well to replicating effective leadership across all twenty five elementary schools so that all of our elementary students can have the same successes regardless of what school attendance area the student resides.

Having a list of what it means to be a leader in Hillsboro who is committed and able to support the needs of all students, but especially ELLs, would help calibrate our leadership team around the district mission and new five year strategic plan. The professional development would look different than what may be occurring in other school districts because the results of this study are unique to Hillsboro.

However, these results do show what principal who were successful did to move their ELLs to a higher level of learning and replicating this work may be worth the effort and professional development investment of time and resources.

Conclusion

Despite 35 years of research about principal leadership and leadership responsibilities, the impact of this critical role and what principals can do to boost ELL student achievement results in a school remains untapped in Hillsboro with the exception of a few schools where the principals reached conclusions on their own.

For principals across the district to be effective leaders for schools with high ELL populations, specific training and coaching using McREL's 21 Leadership Responsibilities needs to be planned and implemented immediately to meet the pressing societal demands for principals who really are motivated, knowledgeable, well trained in effective leadership skills, and highly responsible in moving school systems forward by moving school improvement plans into specific actions that ensure equitable outcomes for all students (see Appendix E).

Only then will no child be left behind and stuck on a road to a life of limited options and poverty.

Each child will have a future and a hope as they begin their lives as college and career ready citizens upon graduation from Hillsboro School District.

REFERENCES

Aleman, D., Johnson Jr., J.F., and Perez, L. (2009). Winning Schools for ELLs. *Educational Leadership, 66*(7), 66-69.

Anuradha, G. A., Brown, Z. A., and Simpson, B. A., (2008). *What does the research say: Research-based characteristics of effective districts, schools, and classroom that promote English learner achievement.* Oakland: WestEd.

Baca, L.M., Fletcher, T., and Hoover, J.J. (2008). Conclusion. Putting the pieces together. In J.K. Klinger, J.J. Hoover, and I.M. Baca (Eds.), *Why do English Language Learners struggle with reading? Distinguishing language acquisition form learning disabilities.* Thousand Oaks: Corwin.

Baker, S. and Baker, D. (2007, September 1). CTL. Retrieved on December 8, 2011 from http://ctl.uoregon.edu/research/projects/set-r.

Baker, S. and Baker, D. (2007, September 1) Reading Intervention with Spanish-Speaking Students: Maximizing Instructional Effectiveness in English and Spanish (SET-R). Retrieved on December 8, 2011 from http://ctl.uoregon.edu/research/projects/set-r.

Bailey, C. A. (2007). *A guide to qualitative field research* (2nd ed.). Thousand Oaks: Pine Forge Press.

Berg, B. L. (2009). *Qualitative research for the social sciences (7th ed.).* Boston: Allyn and Bacon.

Betts, J.R., Reuben, K.S. and Danenberg, A. (2000). *Equal resources, equal outcomes? The distribution of school resources and student achievement in California.* San Francisco: Public Policy Institute of California.

Brownstein, A. (2011). *Waivers and reauthorization of NCLB,* Boston: Thompson Publishing.

Carr, J., and Languloff, R. (2006). *The map of standards for English language learners, K-5.,* San Francisco: WestEd.

Corbin, J. and Strauss, A. (1990). *Basics of qualitative research: Techniques and procedures for developing grounded theory.* San Francisco, CA: Sage Inc.

Cotton, K. (2003). *Principals and student achievement: What the research says.* Alexandria, VA: Association for Supervision and Curriculum Development.

Coulter, G., Shavin, K., and Gichuru, M. (2009). Oral reading fluency: accuracy of assessing errors and classification of readers using a 1-Min time reading sample. *Preventing School Failure, 54*(1), 71-76.

Darling-Hammond, L. (2010). America's commitment to equity will determine our future. *Phi Delta Kappan. 91*(4), 8-14.

Dutro, S. and Helman, L. (2009). *Explicit language instruction: a key to constructing meaning. Literacy Development with English Learners Research-Based Instruction in Grades K-6.* New York: Guilford Publications.

Elmore, R.F. (2000). *Building a new structure for school leadership.* Washington, DC: The Albert Shanker Institute.

Elmore, R.F. (2004). *School Reform from the Inside Out: Policy, Practice, and Performance.* Cambridge: Harvard Education Press.

Fisher, D. and Frey, N. (2008). Releasing. *Educational Leadership, 66*(3), 32-37.

Ford, D., and Whiting, G. (2008). Cultural competence: Preparing gifted students for a diverse society. *Rooper Review, 30*(2), 104-110.

Fullan, M. (2001). *Leading in a culture of change.* San Francisco: Jossey-Bass.

Garcia, G. E. (2000). *Handbook of reading research.* New Jersey: Lawrence Erlbaum and Associates.

Gersten, R., and Baker, S. (2000). What we know about effective instructional practices for English language learners. *Exceptional Children, 66,* 454-70.

Goldenberg, C. N. (2004). *Successful school change: creating settings to improve teaching and learning.* New York: Teachers College Press.

Goldenberg C. N. (2008). Teaching English language learners, what the research does – and does not say. *American Educator, 32*(2), 8-23.

Hanson, M. (2001). Institutional theory and educational change. *Educational Administration Quarterly,* 37(5), 637-661.

Harvey, J. (2011). The school principal as leader: guiding schools to better teaching and learning. *Wallace Perspective,*

Heck, R.H., and Hallinger, P. (2005). The study of educational leadership and management. *Educational Management Administration and Leadership, 33*, 229-244.

Hillsboro Chamber of Commerce. Retrieved February 11, 2012 from http://www.hillchamber.org/.

Hillsboro School District. Retrieved February 11, 2012 from http://www.hsd.k12.or.us/News/NewsArchive/tabid/87/Default.aspx.

Juel, C. (1988). Learning to Read and Write: A Longitudinal Study of 54 Children from First to Fourth Grades. *Journal of Educational Psychology, 88*(4), 437-447.

Kaagan, S. S., and Markle, B. W. (1993). Leadership for learning. *Perspective, 5*(1), 1-16.

Knapp, M.S., Copland, M.A., Honig, M.I., Plecki, M.L., and Portin, B.S. (2010). *Learning-focused leadership and leadership support: meaning and practice in urban systems.* Seattle, WA: University of Washington.

Lashway, L. (2001). Leadership for accountability. *Research Roundup, 17*(3), 1-14. Eugene, ORL Clearinghouse on Education Policy and Management.

Linquanti, R. (2011). *Allocating federal funds for state programs for English language learners.* Washington, DC: The National Academy of Sciences.

Luthens, F. (1988). Successful vs. Effective Real Managers. *Academy of Management Executive, 2*(2): 127-132. Lincoln, University of Nebraska.

Marzano, R.J. (2003). *What works in schools: Translating research into action.* Alexandria: Association for Supervision and Curriculum Development.

Marzano, R. J., Waters, T., and McNulty, B. (2005). *School leadership that works: From research to results.* Aurora, CO: Mid-continent Research for Education and Learning.

Maxwell, J.A. (2005). *Qualitative research design: an interactive approach.* Thousand Oaks: Sage Publications.

McElroy, E. J. (2005). Supporting English Language Learners. *Teaching and Teacher Education, 26,* 679-687.

Menken, K., and Antunez, B. (2001). *An overview of the preparation and certification of teachers working with limited English proficient students.* Washington, DC: The National Clearinghouse for English Language Acquisition.

National Center on Response to Intervention. (2010, January 1). NCRTI. Retrieved July 31, 2011 from http://www.rit4success.org.

National Center for Education Statistics. (2011, January 1). USDOE. Retrieved January 11, 2012 from http://nces.ed.gov/fastfacts/display.asp?id=96.

Neuman, W. L. (2007). *Basics of social research: Quantitative and qualitative approaches (2nd Ed.).* Boston: Allyn and Bacon.

No Child Left Behind Act of 2001 (NCLB), Pub. 1, 107-110, 115 Stat. 1425.

Oregon Department of Education. (2012, January 25). ODE. Retrieved January 26, 2012 from

http://www.ode.state.or.us/news/announcements/announcement.
aspx?ID=7979andTypeID=4.

Oregon Department of Education. (2012, January 19). ODE.
Retrieved January 19, 2012 from
http://www.ode.state.or.us/search/page/?=1389.

Ortiz, A. A. and Graves, A. (2001). Prevention of school failure
and early intervention for
English language learners. In A.J. Artiles and A.A. Ortiz (Eds.),
English Language Learners with special education needs:
identification assessment and instruction. Washington, DC:
Center for Applied Linguistics and Delta Systems Co., Inc.

Powell-Smith, K. A., Good, R. H., and Atkins, T. (2010). *DIBELS*
Next Oral Reading Fluency Readability Study (Tech.
Report No. 7). Eugene, OR: Dynamic Measurement Group.

Reeves, D. B. (2004). *Assessing educational leaders.* Thousand
Oaks: Corwin Press.

Rivera, M. O., Moughamian, A.C., Lesaux, N. K., Francis, D. J.
(2009). *Language and reading*
interventions for English Language Learners and English
Language Learners with disabilities. New Hampshire:
Center on Instruction.

Schlueter, K. and Walker, J. (2008). Selection of school leaders: A
critical component for change.
NASSP Bulletin, 92(1), 37.

Sergiovanni, T.J. (2004). Building a community of hope.
Educational Leadership, 61(8), 33-38.

Silins, H.C., Mulford, W.R., and Zarins, S. (2002). Organizational learning and school change. *Educational Administration Quarterly, 38*(5), 613-642.

Snow, C. E., Burns, M. S., and Griffin, P. (1998). *Preventing reading difficulties in young children.* Washington, DC: National Academy Press.

Supovitz, J.A. (2002). Developing communities of instructional practice. *Teachers College Record, 104*(8), 1591-1626.

Torgesen, J. K., and Wagner, R. K., et al. (1997). Contributions of phonological awareness and rapid automatic naming ability to the growth of word-reading skills in second-to-fifth grade children. *Scientific Studies of Reading, 1*, 161.

Von Frank, V., (2009). Data analysis is a courageous look in the mirror. *The Learning Principal, 5*(2), 1-7.

Wahlstrom, K.L., Louis, K.S., Leithwood, K., and Anderson, S.E. (2010). Investigating the links to improved student learning: *Learning from Leadership Project.*

Waters, T., Marzano, R. J., and McNulty, B. (2003). *Balanced leadership: What 30 years of research tells us about the effect of leadership on student achievement.* Aurora, CO: Mid-continent Research for Education and Learning. Available online at www.mcrel.org.

Wei, R. C., Darling-Hammond, L. Richardson, A. A., and Orphanos, S. (2009). *Professional learning in the learning profession: A status report on teacher development in the United States and abroad.* Oxford: Learning Forward.

Wimpleberg, R., Teddlie, C., and Stringfield, S. (1989). Sensitivity to context: The past and future of effective schools research. *Educational Administration Quarterly, 25*(1), 82-107.

Witziers, B., Bosker, R. J., and Krueger, M. L. (2003). Educational leadership and student achievement: The illusive search for an association. *Educational Administration Quarterly, 39*(3), 398-425.

Wong, L. F. and Snow, C. (2000). *What teachers need to know about language.* Washington, DC: National Academy Press.

Zehr, M.A. (2009). Oral language skills for English learners focus of researchers. *EDWeek, 29*(8),* 8.

APPENDICES

Appendix A: Letter of Informed Consent

Dear Mrs. _____,

As you know, as a former administrator for Hillsboro School District, I am an Oregon educator working with HSD as a principal and District level administrator and I am a doctoral candidate in the Department of Educational Foundations and Leadership at George Fox University in Newberg, Oregon. Per our previous conversations, I am preparing to conduct research for my doctoral dissertation on the role of the principal in improving English Language Learner (ELL) outcomes in Spanish and Reading instruction and to determine whether or not specific principal behaviors have an effect on ELL student outcomes in their respective schools. Specifically, I am trying to gain a fuller understanding of the principals' understanding of the impact of their leadership role on student achievement at their former schools and the work that occurred with the SET-R grant from 2008-2010.

You are being invited to engage in about an hour long personal interview regarding your perceptions and attitudes towards instruction for ELL students, experiences of improving student academic outcomes for ELLs, and evaluation of the leading, teaching, and learning process for ELL students. The questions are fairly general and will relate to your professional background, views on leadership and teaching, professional experiences as an administrator, and post retirement plans. The findings promise to reveal greater insight on the complexities that principals face in guaranteeing a rigorous education for all students especially ELLs. The risks associated with the research are minimal. The personal interview questions are harmless and should not create concern. Nevertheless, please be aware that your participation is completely voluntary and you may decline to continue at any time or decline to answer any question at your will.

The results of this study will only be used for research purposes and may be used for presentations at a professional conference and/ or academic publications. With your permission, personal interviews will be audio recorded and then transcribed at a later time. Information will be analyzed and presented in a confidential manner to that no individual will be personally identified.

All research materials will be filed on a secure computer server and/ or locked in separate, secure locations for up to three years. I will be the only researcher who will have access to any of the materials and after three years I will be responsible for deleting the audio recordings and destroying the relevant materials.

Thank you for taking your time to consider participating in this research project. If you choose to participate, please be aware that you are contributing to further educational leadership. If you have any questions regarding this research, please contact me at (971) 222-6842 or at petersch@hsd.k12.or.us. If you have any further questions, you may contact Dr. Marc Shelton, my GFU Dissertation Board Chair, at (503) 538-8383. Please indicate that you understand the use of this research and agree to participate with your signature below.

Participant Signature

_____

Researcher Signature

_____

Christie M. Petersen

_____

Appendix B: ELL Principal Interview
Guide Questions

Appropriate Probes after a comfortable pause:

1. Tell me more about that please.

2. What do you mean by that?

3. Explore a laugh with "Can you explain that in a little more detail please?"

4. Follow a hunch with "You have been telling me _____, but I get the impression that there is more to your experiences than you are telling me. Is that a fair assessment?

Prompt: "Please tell me _____? Responses:

Prompt	How Prompt applies to knowledge taxonomy
1. What was your college and postgraduate experience like and how did it relate to your role as a principal?	*This addresses Declarative and Procedural knowledge*
2. Why did you choose to become an educator?	*This addresses Experiential knowledge*
3. Why did you choose to become a principal?	*This addresses Contextual knowledge*

4. Have you learned a second language? If so, which one and how.	*This addresses Experiential knowledge*
5. What was your experience like as a teacher?	*This addresses Contextual and Experiential knowledge*
6. What was your experience like as a principal?	*This addresses Contextual and Experiential knowledge*
7. What you believe about student achievement?	*This addresses Experiential knowledge*
8. What you know about best practices in instruction, student engagement, and school culture?	*This addresses Experiential, Declarative, Procedural, and Contextual knowledge*
9. What was the culture at your former school where ELL students were achieving?	*This addresses Contextual knowledge*
10. What events in your school do you think had the most impact on student achievement?	*This addresses Procedural knowledge*
11. What characteristics do principals have to possess to be an effective leader for school improvement, specifically for ELL students?	*This addresses Experiential and Declarative knowledge*

12. How did you improve academic outcomes for ELLs at your school?	*This addresses Experiential, Declarative, Procedural, and Contextual knowledge*
13. What do you think would hinder your work in improving outcomes for ELL students at your school?	*This addresses Declarative and Procedural knowledge*
14. What are the characteristics of a high performing school where ELL students are reaching and exceeding standards towards successful graduation rates?	*This addresses Declarative, Procedural, and Contextual knowledge*
15. Is there anything else you would like to add that we have not discussed?	

Appendix C: The 21 Leadership Responsibilities by Marzano, Waters, and McNulty

What follows are the twenty-one characteristics, defined as responsibilities (2005), for effective leadership. This list has been inserted directly from McREL for easy reference.

1. Culture: fosters shared beliefs and a sense of community and cooperation (r=.29).

2. Order: establishes a set of standard operating procedures and routines (r=.26).

3. Discipline: protects teachers from issues and influences that would detract from their teaching time or focus (r=.24).

4. Resources: provides teachers with materials and professional development necessary for the successful execution of their jobs (r=.26).

5. Curriculum, instruction, assessment: is directly involved in the design and implementation of curriculum, instruction, and assessment practices (r=.16).

6. Focus: establishes clear goals and keeps those goals in the forefront of the school's attention (r=.24).

7. Knowledge of curriculum, instruction, assessment: is knowledgeable about current curriculum, instruction, and

assessment practices (r=.24).

8. Visibility: has quality contact and interactions with teachers and students (r=.16).

9. Contingent rewards: recognizes and rewards individual accomplishments (r=.15).

10. Communication: establishes strong lines of communication with teachers and among students (r=.23).

11. Outreach: is an advocate and spokesperson for the school and all stakeholders (r=.28).

12. Input: involves teachers in the design and implementation of important decisions and policies (r=.30).

13. Affirmation: recognizes and celebrates school accomplishments and acknowledges failures (r=.25).

14. Relationship: demonstrates an awareness of the personal aspects of teachers and staff (r=.19).

15. Change agent: is willing to and actively challenges the status quo (r=.30).

16. Optimizer: inspires and leads new and challenging innovations (r=.20).

17. Ideals/beliefs: communicate and operates from strong ideals and beliefs about schooling ($r=.25$).

18. Monitors/evaluates: monitors the effectiveness of school practices and their impact on student learning ($r=.28$).

19. Flexibility: adapts his or her leadership behavior to the needs of the current situation and is comfortable with dissent ($r=.22$).

20. Situational awareness: is aware of the details and undercurrents in the running of the school and uses this information to address current and potential problems ($r=.33$).

21. Intellectual stimulation: ensures that faculty and staff are aware of the most current theories and practices, and make the discussion of these a regular aspect of the school's culture ($r=.32$).

Appendix D: Synthesis of Research Findings Chart and Notes: The Chemistry of Principal Leadership Characteristics Whose Schools Served ELLs Well

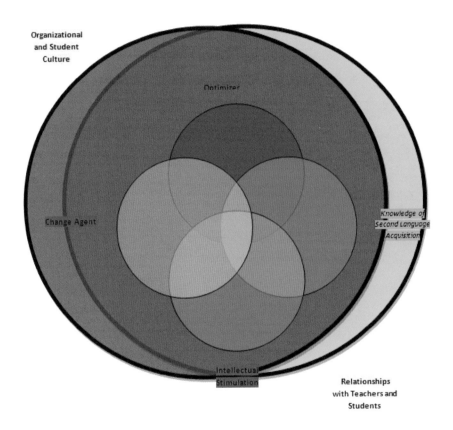

Source: Christie M. Petersen, 2012

- **Chart color coding notes:**
    - ○ McREL's list of leadership responsibilities for second order change that matched with results are highlighted in purple in diagram. These are Intellectual Stimulation, Optimizer, and Change Agent.
    - ○ The two leadership responsibilities that were mentioned by participants but were not part of McREL's list of leadership responsibilities for second order change are highlighted in turquoise in the diagram. These were Knowledge of Second Language Acquisition and Culture. Culture is listed as a leadership responsibility by McREL for first order change, but McREL does not list Knowledge of Second Language Acquisition as part of the 21 leadership responsibilities.
    - ○ One leadership responsibility that was mentioned by participants necessary to be effective with ELLs is Relationships and it is highlighted in grey.
    - ○ McREL's list leadership responsibilities for second order change characteristics that did not match with results are Monitoring/ Evaluating and Flexibility and are not included in diagram.
- **Bottom line:** Based on this research there are half a dozen necessary leadership responsibilities and skills that principals need in order to lead school change to support ELL students. These characteristics are match responsibilities listed by McREL or were mentioned by the principals during the interviews, and are the following:

- o Having extensive knowledge of the Second Language Acquisition process
- o Having strong interpersonal relationships with staff, parents, and students
- o Establishing a Culture where all students are expected to learn and a willingness to do whatever it takes to make that possible for all students
- o Being a change agent
- o Being intellectually stimulating
- o Being an Optimizer by taking advantage of every opportunity to move forward with vision and plan of the school

Appendix E: Winning Schools for English Language Learners in Hillsboro

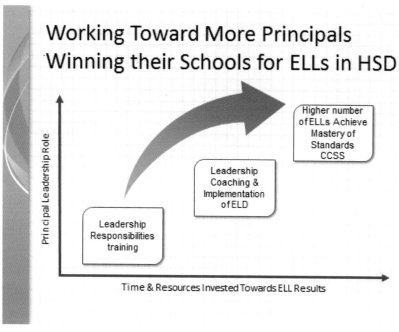

Source: Christie M. Petersen, 2012

Made in the USA
Lexington, KY
12 November 2013